HYPNOSIS INDUCTIONS DISSECTED

JOHN BARBOZA

Edited by
Jane Woodbridge
Christine Ross

Order this book online at www.trafford.com
or email orders@trafford.com

Most Trafford titles are also available at major online book retailers.

© Copyright 2022 John Barboza.
All rights reserved. No part of this publication may be reproduced, stored in a
retrieval system, or transmitted, in any form or by any means, electronic, mechanical,
photocopying, recording, or otherwise, without the written prior permission of the author.

Print information available on the last page.

ISBN: 978-1-6987-1235-2 (sc)
ISBN: 978-1-6987-1237-6 (hc)
ISBN: 978-1-6987-1236-9 (e)

Library of Congress Control Number: 2022913474

Because of the dynamic nature of the Internet, any web addresses or links contained in
this book may have changed since publication and may no longer be valid. The views
expressed in this work are solely those of the author and do not necessarily reflect the
views of the publisher, and the publisher hereby disclaims any responsibility for them.

Any people depicted in stock imagery provided by Getty Images are models, and such
images are being used for illustrative purposes only.
Certain stock imagery © Getty Images.

Cover design by Nskvsky

Trafford rev. 07/20/2022

www.trafford.com

North America & international
toll-free: 844-688-6899 (USA & Canada)
fax: 812 355 4082

CONTENTS

Special Dedication ix
Acknowledgments xi
Foreword xiii
Prelude xv
Introduction xvii
Preface xix
Prestige xxi
Hypnosis xxiii
Induction xxv

Types Of Inductions 1
Types Of Subjects 3
Pre-Talk 5
Conscious / Critical Faculty / Subconscious 7
Hypnotic Contract 9
Safety 11
Observable Hypnotic Indications 13
Deepener 15
Emergence 17
Notes 19

INDUCTIONS

Balloon Induction 23
Wrist Massage Induction 25
Standing Hand Press Induction 27
This Means That Induction 29
One Word Induction 31
Pen And Paper Induction 35
Opposite Induction 37

Three Handshake Induction 39
Waving Hand Induction 43
Hypnogenic Points Induction.....................................45
Clap Induction (Version I) 49
Odd / Even Number Induction 51
False Handshake Induction.......................................53
Warm Hands Induction 55
Eye Exercise Induction 57
Sticky Knees Induction 61
Arm Crawling Induction..63
This Hand / That Hand Induction 67
Be Careful Induction 69
Hand & Eye Induction 71
Clap Induction (Version II)......................................73
Arm Writing Induction...75
Mesmerizing Hands Induction..................................77
Imagine Induction 79
Sensory Pacing Induction..83
The Human Hand Induction....................................85
The Invisible Word Induction 89
Handshake / Arm Induction.....................................95
Clap Induction (Version III) 97
Blackout Induction...99
Déjà Vu Induction 101
Hand Or Eyes Induction.. 103
The Hypnotic Meridian Induction........................... 105
Cycle Of Sleep / Hypnosis Depth Induction 107
Overload Induction 111

Word From The Author 115
About The Author.. 117

A hypnotic induction is a method used to hypnotize someone.

SPECIAL DEDICATION

I dedicate this book to all of the volunteers who permitted me to observe their minds, allowing me to perfect my hypnotic skills.

Thanks to all of the many magnificent hypnotists out there who've created and contributed lots of valuable information to the world. I have appropriated, borrowed, and studied portions of their techniques and ideas that I have incorporated into my own style, which I now have the pleasure of sharing with you.

ACKNOWLEDGMENTS

Special thanks to my mother Patricia, for letting me know, as a child, every time a magician was performing a mystifying magic trick on the television set. My mother's patience was often displayed while I meticulously searched the store-length glass countertop at Cheap John's Joke Shop. I would start at one end, reach the other end, and then backtrack looking for a unique magic trick to purchase and possess as my own.

And thanks to the boy at camp who had everyone talking about the special powers he used to conduct séances, and for scaring me by wiggling his fingers and putting an evil spell on me. I thank him for letting me witness his failed attempt at hypnotizing an eager bystander who appeared to pretend to act like a monkey.

These moments seized the precise elements of wonderment and fear. They fueled and sparked my interests in further exploring the occult, witchcraft, white/black magic, supernatural phenomenon, astral projection, voodoo, zombies, devil possession, religion, and hypnosis.

I zigzagged my way through the dark side, elevating my fears while making sense of my curiosity. This journey has changed my life and is now taking me on a path that is openly revealing the secrets which are deep within us all; secrets that cause turmoil, illnesses, phobias, and fear. It has awakened my inquisitiveness and my desire to search for the truth to better comprehend this mysterious thing we call hypnosis.

In February of 2013, my interest in hypnotism allowed me to cross paths with Master Hypnotist Jeffrey Stephens, the owner, founder, and trainer of the Whole Life Mastery Hypnosis School of the Hypnotic Arts. Jeffrey had a tremendous amount of knowledge to share, and once completing the manuscript for this book; I had planned on asking him to take time out of his busy schedule to contribute his thoughts to the foreword. Sadly, Jeffrey had prematurely passed away before I could proudly share this project with him.

With the blessings of Jeffrey's family, his work is still being taught today by his good friend Master Hypnotist and International Hypnosis teacher, Rudy Nooijen, who worked directly with Jeffrey to learn how to teach the Jeffrey Stephens Hypnosis system that Jeffrey spent years developing. Rudy is keeping Jeffrey's spirit and work alive, and I am honored to have him share his thoughts within the foreword.

FOREWORD

John asked me, in the name of the late Jeffrey Stephens, to write the foreword for his new book on hypnotic inductions. Thank you John, I am honored.

After years of doing hypnotherapy, the hypnosis path personally led me to become an official teacher of the late Master Hypnotist Jeffrey Stephens' work. He is famous for his direct, no-nonsense 15-minute sessions with amazing results. He made an easy 10-step protocol that is being used all around the world, familiar to just about every hypnotist in the field in one way or another.

Having Jeff as a friend and my mentor, I'm sure that he would be proud to have his say in this foreword. He would point out that many inductions and other things within this book can easily be injected in his 10-step protocol. Thanks for this John. While reading this book, I was once again enormously inspired to be even more creative in our wonderful profession.

I personally find this book to be a must-have for all fellow hypnotists, especially since in the art of hypnosis, it can often take many years to really grasp the concept. There are so many factors involved in order to get, for instance, deep and lasting results. However, all these factors that John so beautifully explains in this book become intuitively automatic for any master hypnotist who already possesses the pure knowingness of the hypnotic state. The right intent, mixed with the right expectancy and context, creates this wonderful deep acceptance of the given suggestions in the subconscious mind.

Thank you John, also in the name of Jeff, for reminding the readers that this beautiful pill-free and safe, God-given art is learnable for everyone. It's a great reference book for hypnosis techniques, and also for the sections about safety, the pre-talk, and the hypnotic contract, which I consider to be gems in our field.

Thank you for keeping it so clear, it was a wonderful read. I wish your readers good luck with this hypnosis-inspiring and definitely unique reference-book.

Oh, Jeff would surely add a few of his famous phrases:
"Never Waste A Good Hypnotic State!"
"Always Assume Hypnosis!"

Rudy Nooijen

PRELUDE

I was sitting in the cinema and a woman and four young children were seated in the row in front of me. One of the boys dropped his bag of popcorn and emptied a small amount of the contents on the floor. The woman immediately yelled at him saying, "You're so clumsy. You always drop your popcorn when you are at the movies!" I thought to myself, it's probably because you keep telling him to do so. Was that a suggestion given to him? It had the same elements that hypnosis suggestions have; it contained fear and the shock of being yelled at along with the authoritative commands, "You're so clumsy. You always drop your popcorn when you are at the movies!" I wished I had known when they were going to be at the cinema again so I could see for myself if the same hypnotic suggestion would take place as it did that day.

Another time, a co-worker was being rude. She didn't expect me to yell back at her and when I did, she froze in her spot. Her eyes were fixated on me and her mouth was wide open as if she was petrified. It was as though her brain froze, and she didn't move from that spot until I was done with my long-winded rant. That moment had the unexpected element of surprise, and coupled with the authoritative tone, it seemed to have shocked and immobilized her into a hypnotic statuette.

Another time, I purposely tried an experiment. It was a hectic day and my co-worker needed me to let him out of the room so he could accomplish a few tasks. Overwhelmed and eager to get started with the duties, I opened the door, quickly said, "Here!" and handed him a damp paper towel I had just used to wipe my hands. He froze for several seconds, trying to make sense of the moment. As I started laughing he began to laugh, and I asked him what was going on in his head when I handed him the damp paper towel. He said he wasn't sure and felt like he kind of got stumped for a moment. My thinking is, I disrupted his thought process and his subconscious mind momentarily tried to figure out what to do next. While this was occurring, it stopped him in his tracks and caused a temporary state of confusion. Later I realized I should have followed up with a suggestion.

I look at these events as informal hypnotic inductions where suggestions or instructions were given and all parties were unaware of what was going on. Almost anything can be used as an induction and discovering the simple components required to complete the induction process can be quite astonishing. With this book, my intention is to bring forth many of the elements that appear to be hidden and to make them more recognizable. Once brought to the surface the hypnotic technique can be fine-tuned, making the induction look simplistic and almost magical.

INTRODUCTION

Many years ago I attended a class called Introduction to Criminalistics - Introduction to Criminal Forensics, at Bristol Community College in Fall River, Massachusetts. The first day's homework assignment was for each of the students to look up a gentleman named Louis Pasteur. We were to write a one or two page paper about him and his contributions. While reading, learning, gathering information, and writing about Mr. Pasteur, I quickly understood the reasoning behind the assignment.

Louis Pasteur was a French chemist and microbiologist recognized for his medical discoveries of vaccination, microbial fermentation, and the causes and prevention of diseases. He is best known for his invention of the technique for treating milk and wine known as pasteurization. He is known as the "father of microbiology" because of his numerous discoveries on a molecular level.

Louis Pasteur used powerful microscopes to investigate what the naked eye was unable to see. Studying these tiny elements allowed him to create solutions and eliminate diseases. Through the assignment, I discovered that what Pasteur did is similar to what criminal forensics does. The tiniest of details are sought after and studied, allowing a scientific explanation of what happened, completing the picture and making it possible to understand the dynamics of the situation.

When creating a song in a recording studio, you are learning about how the music is structured. When you hear a song on the radio, you hear the finished product which is comprised of many instruments as well as several voices. Each soundboard, whether it has four tracks or thirty-two tracks, may contain one instrument per track. When you record one instrument at a time on each track, you gain tremendous insight into how the song is created. You are left with a thorough appreciation and understanding of the amount of work that goes into putting a song together. The listening public usually has no clue or isn't concerned about the recording process, but hopefully, they will enjoy the finished product which was painstakingly recorded.

My goal with this book is to do what Louis Pasteur, criminal forensics specialists, and musicians do to understand how and why something works. Seeing a breakdown of the elements that cause the inductions to work helps you to thoroughly understand the process. This gives you the opportunity to become a powerful hypnotist with a collection of reliable and potent tools at your disposal.

PREFACE

This instructional book will explain how to do hypnotic inductions. I will clarify how and why these inductions work. The purpose of this book is to simplify the process and strengthen the reader's ability to understand and perform different induction methods for all types of subjects, ranging from the ultra-suggestible to the refractory.

The easy-to-follow format includes the introduction, the induction, and an explanation of the induction. Each introduction playfully gives you a hint of what the induction entails. The induction is then clearly explained making it easy to follow. The induction explanation further clarifies the procedure.

Note: Sometimes reading instructions or directions can be boring, tiresome to read, and even difficult to comprehend. Along with the above format, another step has been taken to lessen any confusion when discussing the hypnotist and the hypnotic subject. Throughout the book, the male will be addressed as the hypnotist and the female will be addressed as the hypnotic subject.

PRESTIGE

To believe in someone or in someone's ability, you must have faith in that person. That person must be in a commanding position in your mind. When you introduce yourself as a hypnotist, leave no doubt in the other person's mind that you are what you say you are. Your confidence in being a great hypnotist and your confidence in your ability to hypnotize someone must be at its highest level. When you believe in yourself, others will believe in you. The way you present yourself will determine how others see you.

There may be people who will not only discredit you as a hypnotist but refute hypnosis itself. There are believers and nonbelievers. If you wholeheartedly believe in this thing we call hypnosis, stick to your guns, and remain positive, confident, and unfazed to anyone who attempts to deter you. Simply address their issue in one of two ways. The first is to refrain from any further talk about hypnosis with them. There's no sense in trying to persuade someone who refuses to be persuaded. The second is to proceed with a demonstration either with the incredulous person or with someone else altogether. As the demonstration takes place, the skeptic can suddenly become a believer when given a chance to view a hypnosis induction. If the nonbeliever continues to be unfazed, simply revert back to the first option and cease further talk about the matter with that particular person.

When confidence comes from deep within you, it will be picked up subconsciously by others. When people know of your abilities as a hypnotist, there is an aura of context that surrounds you. You have the power of intent when they know that a simple wave of your hand can put them into a deep state of trance or hypnosis. With prestige, you exude confidence, context, intent, knowledge, and a sense of mysticism that radiates from within and grabs the attention of onlookers who can easily be mesmerized by you and your abilities.

HYPNOSIS

Expert practitioners of hypnotism may have varying definitions of what hypnosis is. The following is one of many expressed views.

Hypnosis is a natural human condition that involves a state of heightened awareness, focused attention, and increased response to suggestions.

INDUCTION

An induction is typically a series of instructions used to produce a trance-like state with the intention of evolving into a hypnotic condition. The induction usually involves suggestions to focus, concentrate, and relax. Inductions are used to shift the consciousness of a person from the external environment inwardly. Any situation where we become absorbed in something moves us towards trance and with the right persuasive elements or conditions, hypnosis can occur. And lastly, inductions can come about or be elicited through shock, boredom, fixation of attention, and relaxation.

TYPES OF INDUCTIONS

There are a few types of inductions that are used to induce the trance or hypnotic state. The first is the instant induction that occurs just as fast as saying the word sleep. An unexpected jolt of the arm and the command to sleep followed by a deepener can cause the subject to go into hypnosis.

The next type of induction is the rapid induction. One example would be the "Stress Test" induction where the subject stiffens her entire body while standing with her legs together and her arms down by her sides. When she fails to move her fingers and arms, the inability to lift or move her limbs, along with the hypnotic suggestions, will cause her to drift into hypnosis. Some rapid inductions could take less than a minute to complete while others may take several minutes.

The third type of induction is the slow, progressive, muscle relaxing, body scan induction which is usually done in an office setting. It is also performed in comedy stage hypnosis shows. This kind of induction could take as little as five minutes but may be prolonged for maximum effect. It is a slow process of relaxing the mind, the small and large muscle groups, and the extremities. Visualization suggestions can also be added while comfortably lulling the subject into hypnosis.

With the progressive relaxing technique, a permissive approach is used to persuade the subject into complete physical and mental relaxation. With the instant induction, the authoritative approach is used, and with the rapid induction, a permissive and/or authoritative approach can be used.

Conversational hypnosis techniques or covert hypnosis is when hypnosis is induced through the means of conversation. Covert hypnosis is slightly different in that the subject is unaware or not informed that the hypnotist is using hypnotic techniques to hypnotize her. Powerful hypnotic words, phrases, stories, metaphors, and hypnotic language patterns and techniques are used to induce hypnosis.

TYPES OF SUBJECTS

Some people are extremely susceptible to suggestions while others are not as easily influenced. The individuals who follow instructions easily, without questioning or thinking about why the hypnotist is passively or authoritatively suggesting they do certain things, are the people we call suggestible or hypnotizable. They can easily drift into hypnosis by following simple instructions, sometimes seeming as though they are pretending to be hypnotized because of their quick response.

The individual, who is analytical and verbally or internally questions everything about what is being asked of her, is usually said to be a difficult subject. The person who displays their eagerness to be hypnotized but constantly disobeys the instructions instead of following them would most likely be identified as a refractory subject. With experience, it is fairly easy to identify the eager, manipulative person who appears to have their own agenda for pretending to want to be hypnotized. A simple refusal to hypnotize this type of person can be made by stating, "You seem to be too strong willed at this time. Perhaps a different setting might be a more appropriate time for us to try again."

Occasionally a willing person who is excited to get hypnotized may end up being viewed as a difficult subject, not because of any fault of their own but possibly because the instructions given were not explained clearly. The subject however should always be reminded not to try and make anything happen but instead just let whatever happens, happen.

PRE-TALK

Some hypnotists believe in pre-talks and some don't. When performing comedy stage hypnosis, the hypnotist introduces himself and talks about what the show will be like and what hypnosis is and is not. That is a pre-talk. You can make a pre-talk as long or as short as you'd like, depending on the situation and the type of induction, the time constraints, the location, and whether it is a formal or informal occasion.

In an office setting the hypnotist explains the process of the session and educates the client about hypnosis. This preliminary talk helps put the person in the right frame of mind for the hypnosis session. On the street or stage, the pre-talk should make the person feel excited and eager to be hypnotized. "I'm a hypnotist and I'm going to put you in a deep trance in less than a second." That could be your pre-talk. The question, "Ready to get hypnotized?" could be a pre-talk. Handing your business card out could also be justified as a pre-talk. Expectation is also a key element, so you want the person to anticipate something wonderful happening.

CONSCIOUS / CRITICAL FACULTY / SUBCONSCIOUS

Your conscious mind is the part of the mind you use when you wake up in the morning wondering what you are going to wear, eat, and do etc. It's the analytical, thinking part of your mind. The subconscious mind is the warehouse of your memories. It's the emotional, creative, and fantasy part of your mind. The critical faculty is the passageway into the subconscious mind. It's the firewall that keeps some thoughts out and allows some ideas in through selective thinking (the process where favorable evidence for a particular belief is accepted over unfavorable evidence that may undermine that belief).

When there is a conflict between the conscious and subconscious minds, the subconscious always wins. It is extremely powerful and stores our belief systems, fears, insecurities, behaviors, and strengths, and weaknesses. If you consciously think about quitting smoking and your subconscious mind has many reasons why it believes you should continue smoking, you will have a difficult time trying to quit. If the conscious and subconscious work together and come to an agreement as to why quitting smoking is good for you, you have a better chance of becoming a non-smoker.

When hypnotizing someone with a slow, progressive relaxation induction, you want to preoccupy the conscious mind so that it is either, bored, relaxed, visualizing a scenario, or doing something distracting like counting backwards. With a speed induction you can shock, or confuse them, causing the critical faculty to open the doorway for a split second, allowing access into the subconscious mind. Many examples of these methods will be demonstrated with the following inductions.

HYPNOTIC CONTRACT

A hypnotic contract is when the hypnotist and the subject understand the purpose of the hypnosis event and what it will entail. With the hypnotic contract in place, the subject is ensured the hypnotist will do only what they both agreed upon, therefore ignoring any silly or embarrassing requests from onlookers. Having this hypnotic contract in place builds trust, rapport, and compliance, making the session or event an easy, enjoyable, and positive experience.

SAFETY

The subject's weight or any disabilities should play an important role in considering which types of inductions will be utilized. Knowing this will help you to determine whether or not the subject should be safely seated instead of standing. You wouldn't want to do a standing induction with a taller, heavier subject you may have difficulty controlling if her knees were to buckle under her. You may not be able to prevent injury to her or yourself. It's also important to ask beforehand if she has any injuries that might become aggravated if you were to use a certain induction. An arm pull induction should not be used if she has an arm, wrist, neck, or back injury. Keep in mind there are people with psychological issues that should only be hypnotized by qualified hypnotists, and when hypnotizing minors, permission from parents or guardians should be obtained.

Hypnosis rarely causes side effects or has risks, but note, that you may come across a subject who could experience a headache, drowsiness, or dizziness, after being hypnotized. From my experiences with a subject complaining of a headache, it was always after fractionation was used, a process of repeatedly guiding someone in and out of hypnosis. To remove the headache, I would have her close her eyes and visualize or imagine the headache disappearing. From there I would have her open her eyes of her own accord. One way to eliminate or reduce these experiences from happening is to suggest feelings of the mind being sharp and clear while exiting hypnosis. (See the Emergence section of this book.)

OBSERVABLE HYPNOTIC INDICATIONS

There are a handful of telltale physical signs to look for that will help determine if the subject is entering hypnosis or if she is hypnotized. Her eyes will remain fixated and have a glazed or vacant look to them as though she is looking out into space. Her facial expression will relax. Eye fatigue will cause the eyelids to struggle to remain open, and eye closure, fluttering of the eyelids, lacrimation, and the white of the eyes becoming more noticeable due to the eyeballs rolling upward are also observable signs.

As she becomes more inwardly absorbed she will be oblivious to all outside distractions. Her body and mind will begin to relax as she is overcome with lethargy. Body twitches may occur and noticeable breathing fluctuation may take place. An increase in her pulse rate and respiration along with swallowing may occur as she is entering hypnosis. Her breathing will slow down and swallowing may appear to stop while hypnotized. Her body may remain still and muscular activity, if any, such as movement of the limbs, may be sluggish.

During hypnosis there may be a delay in response to suggestions. When emerging from hypnosis, the subject may feel slightly disoriented. She may yawn, stretch, feel overly relaxed, calm, tired, and even sleepy. Some subjects may feel as though they didn't get hypnotized at all, in fact, they may even mention that they fell asleep. But of course, an experienced hypnotist will realize these responses are all observable, physical indications of a hypnotic experience.

DEEPENER

A deepener is a method used to cause the subject to enter a highly suggestible state deep enough that responses to positive suggestions will be achieved. Once the induction is completed it is critical to quickly follow up with the deepener. The deepener can be as simple as saying, "Go deeper and deeper and deeper down."

The slow progressive relaxation induction can also be used as a deepener. The subject is directed to mentally scan the entire body focusing on relaxing the muscles in the feet all the way up to the head or vice versa. An example would be as follows. "Focus all of your attention on both of your feet. Each time you inhale and exhale, imagine the relaxation moving upward relaxing your ankles and then your shins, and your calves, knees, and so forth. By the time you reach your head, your entire body will be completely relaxed."

A more traditional deepening method is having the subject visualize walking down a staircase of a set amount of steps while being given suggestions to relax. With each movement downward the subject is persuaded to enter a deeper state of relaxation.

Deepeners can also be used throughout the hypnotic experience to deepen the hypnotic state to a depth where the subject becomes more open and receptive to suggestions for change. Short suggestions telling the subject to simply go deeper into hypnosis can sporadically be used.

EMERGENCE

When you are ready to have the subject emerge from hypnosis, you can simply count from one to three. On the count of three, tell her to open her eyes and return to the room feeling good in every way. You can count from one to five or ten if you prefer. A good rule of thumb is to ease the subject out of hypnosis, starting out slowly, picking up the pace, and slightly increasing the volume or intensity giving her a gift of wonderful, positive suggestions as you count her out of hypnosis.

Here is one example of emerging a subject from hypnosis. "As I begin counting from one to five, each and every number will bring you closer to full conscious awareness. By the time I reach the number five you will be wide awake, feeling absolutely wonderful in every way, shape, and form. One... take a deep breath feeling relaxed. Two... stretching, feeling wonderful as your mind becomes fully alert. Three... your body and mind feeling energized with every breath. Four... eyes beginning to open, feeling wonderful, fantastic, energized and Five... eyes wide open, feeling calm, alert, comfortable, energized and absolutely fantastic."

NOTES

Always ask for permission to hypnotize anyone. It builds trust and is the ethical and professional thing to do.

At times during the induction, you may have to touch the subject's hands, wrists, shoulders, face, or head. Some people do not like to be touched so it's important to ask for their permission beforehand.

With each induction, after giving the command to sleep or go into hypnosis, immediately follow up with a deepener.

Always keep in mind the number one priority which is the safety of the subject. Be aware of any injuries and be sure to prevent injuries from occurring.

Patter is the way you speak or the way you say things in a rapid fire mechanical manner. Some of the inductions include patter which you can memorize and repeat verbatim. Others will require you to create your own interesting chattering talk which preludes or accompanies the induction.

It may be required to repeat or prolong certain sections of some inductions or it may be required to repeat entire inductions more than once in order to induce hypnosis.

INDUCTIONS

BALLOON INDUCTION

Introduction:

Balloons come in all shapes and sizes, are made of different materials, and serve many purposes ranging from sports, recreation, science, medicine, military, and even hypnosis.

Induction:

Relay to the subject in a smooth, continuous, slightly authoritative tone, "Imagine an invisible balloon right here." While saying this, place your cupped hands together with the sides of your index fingers touching each other and the sides of your thumbs naturally touching each other. Your palms should be facing the floor and the back of your hands should be facing the ceiling. Both hands should be cupped as if you are holding the top of an inflated invisible balloon. As the hands separate, the left hand should arch its way down from the top and left side of the balloon. The right hand should simultaneously move and arc downward from the top and right side meeting the left hand at the bottom center of the balloon. The sides of your pinkies should now be touching each other. The palms should be facing the ceiling and the back of your hands should be facing the floor. Continue on by saying, "Imagine this invisible balloon has a force field around it." Place your hands on the right and left sides of the balloon as you mimic trying to squeeze it, and say, "You cannot penetrate this force field.

Put your hands here." Assist the subject by placing her palms on each side of the invisible balloon, making sure her wrists, elbows, and shoulders are locked in place and her stiff fingers are spread apart displaying a slight curvature to them. "Close your eyelids and imagine seeing the balloon. When you can see the balloon in your mind, tell me what color it is." The moment she tells you what color the balloon is, immediately tell her to try and pop the balloon by saying, "You cannot penetrate that force field. Try and pop that balloon now. Try and penetrate that force field, you cannot." The moment her hands struggle to squeeze the balloon, exclaim, "Try harder." Without hesitation loudly clap your hands together, and in a commanding voice say, "Sleep!"

Explanation:

As previously mentioned, the following should be said in a slightly authoritative tone from start to finish. "Imagine an invisible balloon right here. Imagine this invisible balloon has a force field around it. You cannot penetrate this force field. Put your hands here, close your eyelids, and imagine seeing the balloon. When you can see the balloon in your mind, tell me what color it is. You cannot penetrate that force field. Try and pop that balloon now. Try and penetrate that force field, you cannot. Try harder. Sleep!" The continuous flow of instructions and commands leaves no room for intrusive thoughts or doubts to surface. Locking the fingers, wrists, elbows, and shoulders in place makes it difficult to successfully squeeze the balloon. The moment the subject sees the balloon in her mind's eye and tells you what color it is, indicates that selective thinking has occurred. The physical struggle to pop the balloon is proof that the critical faculty has been bypassed. The loud clap of your hands (popping of the balloon) accompanied by your command to sleep startles the subject, causing her to immediately enter hypnosis.

WRIST MASSAGE INDUCTION

Introduction:

Massage therapy is used to relieve stress, promote relaxation, reduce muscle tension, and relieve headaches and migraines. This particular wrist massage is used to create muscle tension and induce hypnosis.

Induction:

Have the subject turn her hand over so that her palm is facing upward towards the ceiling and the back of her hand is facing the floor. Her arm should be bent with her elbow and bicep leaning against her ribs, and her hand should be out in front of her. With your index finger, gently massage the palmaris longus muscle, located at the center of her wrist at the base of her hand. Tell her to stare at her palm and to pay particular attention to how the caressing of her wrist causes her fingers and thumb to fully separate from each other by stretching and extending outward. Tell her to notice how the skin of her palm tightens, spreading and locking the fingers, causing the entire hand to become stiff and rigid. Tap her palm and fingers to show her how taut her hand has become. Continue caressing her wrist and have her try to bend the weakest finger and then another. After failing to bend her fingers, tell her that her entire hand is so stiff and rigid that she is unable to close her hand into a fist. Tell her to try. After attempting to close her hand, tell her that as soon as you tap the middle of her palm, her hand will automatically close. Let her know that as her fingers close into a fist her eyelids will also close. Tap her palm and convince her that her fingers and eyelids are now tightly closing and locking in place. The moment she closes her fist and eyelids, proceed with a deepener. Suggest that she relaxes all tension in her eyes, hand, and body as she goes deeper into hypnosis.

Explanation:

The subject's ability to follow your simple instructions of adjusting her hand and arm into position exhibits compliancy. Focusing her attention on the center of her palm helps her to remove and ignore all outside stimuli. It also helps to guide her inwardly. Your suggestions along with the massaging of the wrist aids in bypassing her critical faculty, which makes it easy to produce hypnotic phenomena or hypnosis.

STANDING HAND PRESS INDUCTION

Introduction:

This rapid induction will amazingly send the subject off to hypnosis-bliss before she even has a chance to sit down and get comfortable.

Induction:

With both you and the subject facing each other, have her stand with her feet shoulder-width apart, the same way you are standing. From there, have her lightly place the palm of her left hand on top of your right palm which is in front of you, facing the ceiling, and located at chest level. As you point to your eyes with your left hand, tell her to look into your eyes and focus. Place your left hand on her right shoulder, look down at your shoes, and have her look downward also. As you adjust your feet a few different ways before finding the right position, instruct her to do the same. While this is taking place you should undetectably be removing your right hand from its location, positioning your hand so that the palm is now facing the floor and is closely above her hand. During the final positioning of your feet, simultaneously and swiftly press down on the back of her hand while snapping the fingers of your left hand near her face, as you command her to sleep.

Explanation:

While conducting the pre-induction instructions, remember that with all standing hypnotic inductions, safety should be briefly discussed simply by stating to the subject that she will maintain her balance throughout the entire hypnotic experience. Observe the compliance of the subject by guiding and instructing her to position herself closely in front of you. From there, the palm to palm placement instructions are given. Having her gaze into your eyes and focus, adds an element of curiosity and anticipation. Placement of your hand on the subject's shoulder assists in moving her into the correct standing position, and it adds to the hypnotic experience by including the kinesthetic sense. The next set of instructions fully preoccupies her attention as you demonstrate how you want her to properly position her feet to maintain her balance. It's just the right amount of diversion needed for you to surprise her by pressing her floating hand downward and shocking her by snapping your fingers close to her face and commanding her to sleep.

THIS MEANS THAT INDUCTION

Introduction:

If this means that, and that means this, then that will happen because of this and vice versa.

Induction:

After telling the subject to sit comfortably, have her close her eyelids and tell her the following. "Whenever I say sleep, think of it as deep relaxation and whenever I say relax, think of it as deep sleep. Okay?" When she responds in the affirmative tell her to open her eyelids and focus on an object in front of her. Have her take a few slow, deep, breaths. During each exhalation tell her to sleep. During the last exhalation tell her to sleep and relax. Pause for several seconds and have her begin taking a few more slow, deep, breaths, telling her to sleep during each exhalation. During the last exhalation tell her to sleep and relax her legs. Briefly pause and then have her continue with the slow, deep, breaths while telling her to sleep during each exhalation. During the last exhalation tell her to sleep, relax, and go deeply to sleep as she allows her arms to relax. Briefly pause and have her take a few more breaths while telling her to sleep during each exhalation. During the last exhalation tell her to sleep, and relax deeply as her body and mind relaxes with every breath. As you monitor her normal breaths tell her to sleep every time she inhales and to deeply relax every time she exhales. It may be necessary to coax her into letting her heavy eyelids sleep and relax. The moment she closes her eyelids, reinforce deep sleep and deep relaxation.

Explanation:

Having the subject think of sleep when telling her to relax and having her relax when telling her to sleep is a great relief for the hypnotist. There's nothing more disconcerting than watching a subject keep her eyes open after telling her to sleep. With this induction, you can tell her to sleep as long as you need to without worrying about eye closure. The word sleep should become synonymous with the word relax while also doubling as a suggestion to go into a hypnotic sleep. The word relax should become synonymous with the word sleep while also doubling as a suggestion to relax. Any confusion between the two words helps to move her towards experiencing the effects of becoming relaxed and going into hypnosis. The slow, deep, rhythmic breathing relaxes her, and the soft soothing repetition of the words sleep and relax guides her into hypnosis. Her fixed gaze tires the eyes, and her fatigued eyelids alerts you to implement eye closure, something often looked at as part of the hypnotic experience, which usually causes the subject to believe something hypnotic is occurring.

ONE WORD INDUCTION

Introduction:

Words are extremely powerful; they form our belief systems, motivate us, and can emotionally impact our lives. Imagine using one word to start the process for change.

Induction:

Begin by telling the subject, "I once read that, 'Eye closure is the opening wedge to hypnosis.'" Now say, "So close your eyelids." Continue on by telling her, "There is a one-word induction that instantly causes someone to close their eyelids and go deeply into hypnosis. It happens so quickly that almost everyone who experiences it is amazed." Ask the subject, "If there was one word that you would want to hear that illustrates the meaning of what hypnosis is to you, a word that would instantly put you into hypnosis, what word would you choose to instantly go deeply into hypnosis? Think of a word that relates to hypnosis and imagine the sound of that word making you feel very relaxed, so relaxed that the moment you hear it, your eyelids immediately close, and your body instantly becomes completely loose, limp, and relaxed. In your mind say and hear that word - now- imagine instantly closing your eyelids and going deeply into hypnosis." Pause for a moment as she imagines saying the word, closing her eyelids, and going into hypnosis. Repeat, "Again, think of that word that relates to hypnosis and imagine the sound of that word making you feel very relaxed, so relaxed that the moment you hear it, your eyelids immediately close, and your body instantly becomes completely loose, and limp, and relaxed. In your mind say and hear that word - now- imagine instantly closing your eyelids and going deeply into hypnosis." Pause for a moment as she imagines saying the word, closing her eyelids, and going into hypnosis. Continue on by saying, "Let your feet relax... Relax your legs... Relax your thighs... and your stomach. Let your chest relax with every breath in... and every breath out... relax... relax... relax your upper and lower back as you breathe... and relax your arms and your hands. Now let your head relax... let the muscles in your neck and face relax... relax... relax your entire body and mind with every breath that you take... now think of that word and imagine the sound of that word making you feel very relaxed, so relaxed that the moment you hear it, your eyelids immediately close, and your body instantly becomes completely loose, limp, and relaxed. Now say the word out loud." The moment she says the word out loud, say, "Close your eyelids and go deeply into hypnosis now!" Pause for a moment as she imagines closing her eyelids and instantly going deeply into hypnosis. Tell her, "Let your feet relax... Relax your legs... Relax your thighs... and your stomach. Let your chest relax with every breath in... and every breath out... relax... relax... relax your upper and lower back as you breathe... and relax your arms and your hands. Now let your head relax... let the muscles in your neck and face relax... relax... relax your entire body and mind... each time you say that word... you go into hypnosis quicker and deeper." Continue with the suggestions by saying, "In a moment I'm going to have you open your tired, relaxed, heavy eyelids, and the moment you open your tired, relaxed, heavy, eyelids, say the word out loud, and go deeply into hypnosis. Go deeper and quicker than the other times. Open your eyelids, say the word out loud, and go deeply into hypnosis now!"

Explanation:

Having the subject choose a word personalizes the meaning of that word and gives it the power to cause hypnosis to occur. Having her practice imagining saying and hearing the word, and visualizing herself going into hypnosis, primes her to react the same way when the final command is given. During the very last sentence after you tell her to open her eyelids, the moment she opens her eyelids tell her to say the word. The moment she says the word and closes her eyelids, give her the command to go deeply into hypnosis.

PEN AND PAPER INDUCTION

Introduction:

When using writing utensils to inscribe something formal or informal, our kinesthetic, auditory, visual, and sometimes olfactory senses are utilized. This induction hones in on a particular sense in order to induce hypnosis.

Induction:

Have the subject close her eyelids and listen to the sound of the writing tool rapidly scribbling an oblong pattern on a blank sheet of paper. As the subject listens and acknowledges that she hears the rhythmic sound, continue with the suggestions to sleep as the sound slows and fades away.

"Close your eyelids and just listen to the hypnotic sound that the pen and paper make... Is it the pen making the sound...? Or is it the paper causing the sound...? Perhaps it could be the ink splashing on the paper as the pen moves back and forth... back and forth... back and forth... creating the relaxing, soothing, hypnotic sound... as you breathe in and out... in and out... in and out... as you relax... and breath... relax... and breath... relax... and breath... back and forth... back and forth... back and forth... breathing... listening... fading away... fading away... fading away... as you go deeper and deeper into hypnosis... sleep... breath... relax... and go deeper and deeper down... down... down."

Explanation:

The hypnotic sound of the nib of the pen against the paper in harmony with the soft, soothing, suggestions to relax, listen, breathe, and sleep is all that is needed for this auditory induction to produce hypnosis.

OPPOSITE INDUCTION

Introduction:

If you think it's confusing enough to try and follow instructions, just wait and see how confusing trying *not* to follow instructions can be.

Induction:

Articulate to the subject, "In order to be hypnotized, it is extremely important to follow simple instructions. In order for you to follow the instructions I am about to give you, you must place your undivided attention on my requests because you have to do the opposite of everything I tell you to do. So if I tell you to blink - don't blink, or if I tell you not to blink - blink." Test the subject to see if she understands by telling her to blink. If she doesn't blink tell her not to blink. Once she blinks and demonstrates that she understands, continue by telling her to open her eyelids. She will close her eyelids. Tell her to close her eyelids. She will open her eyelids. Have her exhale. She will inhale. Tell her to inhale. She will exhale. Now tell her to open her eyelids. When she closes her eyelids, in an authoritative voice immediately command her to sleep by saying, "And don't - Sleep!" as you gently but firmly touch her forehead.

Explanation:

Explaining to the subject what she must do in order to get hypnotized helps to clarify what she shouldn't do. It also is a way of setting up the induction in her mind and helps eliminate any questions. Reiterating the instructions by testing her before starting the induction will help build her confidence. Complimenting her for successfully passing the test reassures her that she is quite capable of following instructions and is ready to successfully be hypnotized. When telling the subject to blink, she is expected not to blink. Allow a few brief seconds to pass to carefully prolong the time period before giving the next directive to not blink, which will prompt her to blink. While hesitating during this brief time period, if you wait too long, she may find it difficult to refrain from blinking. You want to extend the time frame after telling her to blink long enough for her to be mentally concerned about blinking, while physically struggling to not blink. And then you want to tell her not to blink so she can release the tension and blink.

During the induction when she closes her eyelids after you tell her to open them, pause for approximately fifteen seconds allowing her to relax and experience the calm, peaceful moment. This will also allow her to anticipate the next instruction. From here on pick up the pace and rattle off the consecutive suggestions. Tell her to close her eyelids. As soon as she opens them have her inhale by telling her to exhale. Seconds before allowing her to completely fill her lungs with air have her exhale by telling her to inhale. In the middle of her exhalation tell her to open her eyelids which she will close. Immediately command her to sleep by softly saying, "And don't…" and raise your tone when saying, "…Sleep!" as you gently but firmly touch her forehead. The pacing will help to keep things flowing while limiting or removing any internal dialogue that could get in the way of successfully completing the induction. It also causes a slight amount of confusion which helps to increase the subject's anticipation for hypnosis to occur.

THREE HANDSHAKE INDUCTION

Introduction:

This is a great induction to use on anyone who may not be completely comfortable getting hypnotized but wants to at least give it a try. It is a simple induction and by the time you explain the process to the person, you will have already drawn them halfway into the hypnotic state. And before they know it, they will instantly find themselves pleasantly experiencing the wonderful phenomenon of hypnosis.

Induction:

While the subject is sitting comfortably with both feet flat on the floor with her hands and arms resting on her lap, begin by saying, "I'm going to explain exactly what we are going to do while taking you through the motions. After I explain and show you what we are going to do, we will proceed with the induction and you will find yourself in a wonderful state of hypnosis. Okay?"

From here on physically go through the motions while explaining the process. "The first thing I'm going to do is have you stare directly into my eyes and focus." As she gazes into your eyes, shake her hand as you continue on. "Then I am going to shake your hand while you take a slow deep breath, hold it for a few seconds, and exhale." Somewhere between holding her breath and exhaling, stop shaking her hand, but remain holding it throughout the entire induction. After the completion of her exhalation, begin shaking her hand as you continue on. "Then I'm going to shake your hand again as you take another slow deep breath now, hold it for a few seconds, and exhale." Again, somewhere between holding her breath and exhaling, stop shaking her hand but remain holding it. After the completion of her exhalation continue on by saying, "I'm going to shake your hand once more, but this time I want you to take an even slower... deeper... breath now..." Begin shaking her hand. "...hold it for a few seconds, close your eyelids, and exhale..." Somewhere between holding her breath and exhaling, stop shaking her hand but remain holding it. "...then I will say, 'sleep' and you will go into a deep relaxing wonderful hypnotic sleep. Okay?" After she acknowledges, if her eyes are still closed have her open them.

Now begin the hypnotic process by telling her to stare directly into your eyes. Shake her hand and tell her to take a slow, deep, breath, hold it for a few seconds and exhale. Somewhere between holding her breath and exhaling, stop shaking her hand. As she remains fixated on your eyes, shake her hand a second time as you tell her to take another slow, deep, breath, hold it for a few seconds, and exhale. Again, somewhere between holding her breath and exhaling, stop shaking her hand and continue holding on to it. For the third and final time, shake her hand and say, "Take a slow... deep... breath, hold it for a few seconds..." As she holds her breath stop shaking her hand. "...and exhale as you close your eyelids." Immediately after the subject closes her eyelids, firmly tug her arm, while placing your left hand on her shoulder or head as you command her to sleep.

Explanation:

The instructions and physical demonstration primes the subject's subconscious mind with what will be taking place during the hypnotic induction. Explaining in easy-to-follow directions shows the subject what is expected to happen and prepares her to completely comply, lessening or omitting any thoughts of resistance. Through repetition, knowing exactly what to do makes it easy for the subject to readily go along with every step of the process. The dry run causes the subject to become comfortable and gives her a sense of readiness to follow the instructions correctly. To the subconscious mind, it's as if everything you're doing or about to do has already been done. It's familiar and therefore the subject automatically responds.

When you have her exhale, use your hand to motion her to close her eyelids. A slow downward wave of your left hand near and past her eyes, visually instructs her to close her eyelids. As Ormond McGill mentioned in his book titled, The New Encyclopedia of Stage Hypnotism, "Eye closure is the opening wedge to hypnosis." It also eliminates outside visual stimuli preparing the subject for her inward journey.

Instant rapport is gained when telling the subject that a full explanation and demonstration will take place before the induction process is even started. Demonstrating every detail preps the subject and allows you to ease any nervousness and make any needed corrections. When you have the subject stare into your eyes, you are also fixating your gaze directly into her eyes. When the subject is asked to inhale deeply, you should be demonstrating how to inhale by inhaling deeply and holding your breath also. When you shake the subject's hand, you will be able to know if you are in complete control of the handshake. If she is shaking your hand, you must remind her to just relax and let you do all the work. You will also know if she is tense or relaxed. If the subject's arm is stiff and tense, instruct her to relax her arm muscles. Several attempts to loosen the arm may be needed. Softly wiggling her arm back and forth and explaining that all she has to do is let her arm become loose and limp, should sufficiently remove the tension. Once the corrections are made and understood, continue on by shaking her hand, reminding her to look into your eyes, and to inhale and exhale.

As you take hold of the subject's hand, tell her to stare into your eyes. Eye fixation helps keep the subject focused on a point which helps to eliminate any surrounding distractions, but even more importantly, prolonged absorption in a single idea helps bypass the critical faculty. Looking upward into your eyes, while she is sitting down, also causes the eyes to quickly tire.

The handshakes during both the explanation of what's going to occur and during the hypnotic process should be casually relaxed. All the handshakes should slow down just before coming to a complete stop. The third and very last handshake during the induction process should slow down and then end with the tugging of the arm. The unexpected tug and command to sleep is the key to causing the subject to abruptly become completely relaxed while quickly entering hypnosis.

WAVING HAND INDUCTION

Introduction:

You can wave hello or goodbye to someone, or you can wave at somebody to come closer or to get their attention. You can even wave at someone to hypnotize them.

Induction:

While greeting the subject and moving your opened hand forward to shake hers, redirect your hand upward in front of her face while taking hold of her shoulder with your left hand. Gently rock her side to side as you slowly and continuously wave your right hand side to side in the opposite direction of her body movement, while blurting out the following suggestions for her to obey. "Look at my hand and relax - as you keep looking at my hand go deeper into hypnosis - as you close your heavy eyelids go even deeper into hypnosis - now - relax... and go deeper... deeper... down."

Explanation:

Motioning to shake the subject's hand and avoiding it altogether constitutes a handshake interrupt induction, which triggers her to try and make sense of what just happened. Before she has a chance to engage in her thoughts, she is directed to focus her attention on your hand as it waves from side to side in front of her face. The nonstop suggestions, the swaying of her body, and her fascination with your palm movement fully engages her attention. When you say, "…go even deeper into hypnosis…" momentarily stop moving your hand and rocking her body. Immediately resume rocking her body from side to side as you carry on with the rest of the suggestions to go deeper into hypnosis.

As previously mentioned, the non-contact handshake interrupt induction or false handshake, momentarily causes the subject to try and make sense of what just happened. This allows you to bypass her critical faculty with your continuous suggestions, which keeps her mind focused on your voice and words, and reduces any conscious awareness. Moving her body to the left while waving your hand towards the right, and then shifting her body to the right while waving your hand to the left, causes her to struggle to keep her eyes fixated on your palm. This visual and tactile swaying motion also stimulates the equilibrium which is another component that contributes to guiding her into hypnosis. Abruptly stopping all motion, momentarily pausing, resuming, and then finally completing the suggestions as a run-on sentence, interrupts the swaying movement, reinstates it, adds a little confusion, and quickly sends her deeper into hypnosis.

HYPNOGENIC POINTS INDUCTION

Introduction:

Once you familiarize yourself with the hypnogenic points, you will be able to use this incredibly powerful induction to instantly zap the subject into hypnosis.

Induction:

Start out by saying, "This is one of my favorite inductions. I love doing this induction because it is very powerful. I only use this induction on people who I know will go into hypnosis instantaneously and deeply. There are three points located on the face which we call the hypnogenic points. Like I said earlier, I only use this induction on people who go into hypnosis instantaneously and very deeply. I would never use it on anyone who doesn't go into hypnosis quickly because I wouldn't want any problems. All I do is put my three fingers on these three points on the face and - sleep!"

Explanation:

You can explain this induction to a third party who is there to observe, but you may also explain it directly to the subject if there aren't others present. As you may have noticed, the induction paragraph is explained as a precondition, where in fact the entire explanation of this induction is actually the induction itself. If explaining this induction to a third party, the subject is sitting quietly listening and taking in all that is being said. This indirect induction method starts out with you saying, "This is one of my favorite inductions because it is very powerful."

The next line, "I only use this induction on people who I know will go into hypnosis instantaneously and deeply," is what causes the subject to go into hypnosis instantaneously and deeply. What's happening here is the subject has been indirectly given the suggestion that this induction will cause her to go into a deep state of hypnosis very quickly.

The next part that follows is the explanation of the hypnogenic points located on the face. There really isn't any such thing as a hypnogenic point, but for this induction, you will assure anyone listening that there is. Just the belief is all that is needed in order for the subject to instantaneously enter a deep state of hypnosis once the three points on the face are touched.

In this next phase of the induction, you reiterate your concern about why you only use this induction on certain subjects. Again, the concern is that anyone who doesn't get hypnotized quickly and deeply may end up with problems, and that is why you only use this induction on subjects that you know will go into hypnosis quickly and deeply. The subject presumes that she is that certain person who can go into hypnosis extremely quickly and deeply because you're going to demonstrate this induction on her.

You don't mention what the problems are, but you do mention that there could be problems. This leaves the subject with just enough information to make her wonder, but not enough information to be of any concern. After all, she has just been reassured that she is a good subject who easily goes into hypnosis instantaneously and deeply, therefore there will be no problems if she follows the suggestions given. By the way, there really aren't any concerns about problems arising, but for this induction, you will make sure that anyone listening believes that there are legitimate concerns.

All that is needed now is the touching of the three areas on the face to immediately send the anticipating subject into a deep state of hypnosis. When you begin to show the third party or the lone subject how it works, you should be positioning your three fingers inches away from her face while saying, "All I do is put my three fingers on the three points on the face and - sleep!" Simultaneously put your three fingers on her face when you say "sleep!" Quickly, gently, and safely place the thumb and ring finger below the eyes and the index finger on the forehead between the eyes.

CLAP INDUCTION (VERSION I)

Introduction:

The simple act of the subject clapping her hands together is enough for her to enter hypnosis.

Induction:

Have the subject stand to your side as you relay the following instructions to her. "When I count to three you will clap your hands like this and go into hypnosis." Demonstrate the entire procedure to the subject while explaining, "With your arms down by your sides, when I begin counting, starting with the number one, bend your left arm and lift your hand about shoulder level." Your palm should be facing your right side. "When I say the number two, bend your right arm and lift your hand in front of you also about shoulder level." Your palms should be facing each other. "When I say the number three, quickly bring those hands together making one loud clap." After demonstrating what is required of the subject, have her put her arms down by her sides. Tell her to look forward and to stare at something for a moment as you advise her to slowly inhale and exhale a few times. After the completion of the breaths, briefly pause as she continues focusing her attention on the object in front of her. Firmly say the number one. The moment she bends her arm and positions her left hand out in front of her body say the number two. As soon as she lifts her right hand in position, count out the number three and immediately place your palm over her face and eyes while commanding her to sleep. She may have time to clap her hands but most likely they will drop down before she has a chance to complete the clap as she enters hypnosis.

Explanation:

The combination of catching the subject off guard by interrupting her handclap, and startling her by unexpectedly covering her eyes and face with your hand is an effective way to bypass the critical faculty. Startling her causes her subconscious mind to take notice, and commanding her to sleep is all that is needed for her to enter hypnosis.

ODD / EVEN NUMBER INDUCTION

Introduction:

When concentrating on opening and closing the eyes and counting and staring at an object, it's just a matter of time before sleep overcomes the subject - almost as quickly as the blink of an eye.

Induction:

Have the subject sit and focus her attention on an object. Tell her you will count out the numbers one and two. Every time you say the number one, she is to close her eyelids, and every time you say the number two, she is to open her eyelids. Tell her that when you say the number two, she is to keep her eyes focused on the object, and when you say the number one, she is to continue fixating her tightly closed eyelids in the direction of the object. Once she indicates that she understands, begin counting and mentioning that every time she closes her eyelids, she will find it harder to open them and even harder to keep them open. As you continue counting, carry on by telling her how tired her eyes are becoming and how heavy her eyelids are getting. Before you know it, her eyelids will remain closed and you will have the opportunity to tell her to sleep.

Explanation:

When the subject is sitting and focusing her attention on the object, the idea is to have her gaze upward, preferably slightly above eye level. This, along with explaining the process to her in a deliberately slow fashion, will cause the eyes to quickly tire. After signaling to you that she understands what to do, begin counting. Start out by normally saying one. Let the eyelids stay closed for several seconds before saying the number two. Immediately after saying two, have the eyelids quickly close by rapidly saying one. You want the eyelids to stay closed a little longer than staying open, but you also want to watch for eye fatigue when they are open so that you can actually see the heaviness of the eyelids increasing. In a short time, you should notice the eyelids struggling to remain open. When you see that great effort is needed to open them, mix the numbers up by saying one, then saying one again, and then two. You can also say the word sleep in between the numbers. And of course, while counting you should also be interjecting how heavy the eyelids have become, how tired the eyes are, and that the eyelids are so tired and heavy that the subject is finding them harder to open and easier to close.

FALSE HANDSHAKE INDUCTION

Introduction:

As the hypnotist approaches the subject to greet her with a handshake, she is suddenly swooped into a hypnotic state before the formal greeting ever takes place.

Induction:

As you approach the subject, extend your right hand out towards her as though you are attempting to shake her hand. As she extends her hand towards yours, bring both of your hands up towards the subject's face. Lightly grasp both sides of her head and command her to sleep.

Explanation:

This handshake induction is interrupted before the hands ever get to meet. Avoiding the handshake altogether, invading her personal space, enveloping her face with your cupped hands, and adding a direct, authoritative command to sleep, is more than enough to startle and cause her to follow your simple directive.

WARM HANDS INDUCTION

Introduction:

One physical attribute that signifies suggestibility and the receptivity of hypnotic suggestions is having warm hands.

Induction:

Gently take hold of the subject's wrists and bring her hands out in front of her so that both palms are touching each other. Direct her to quickly rub the palms together as you mention how the hands will immediately begin getting warm. Ask her if she notices the heat radiating within and between the palms. Once she answers in the affirmative, tell her to try and keep rubbing them together as she closes her eyelids and imagines the hands continually getting hotter as she presses them tightly together. Tell her that the friction will begin to increase the heat and cause her hands to get sticky as if there is hot glue melting and sealing the palms tightly together. Have her notice how the sliding hand movement is slowing down, causing the palms to meld together and lock in place. The moment the hands stop moving, tell her they are locked together and she cannot unstick them. Have her try and pull them apart. Tell her that as she tries and realizes how difficult it is to separate her hands, it causes her to go into hypnosis. Have her take notice of how the downward movement of her hands indicates that she is quickly going deeper into hypnosis.

Explanation:

Telling the subject to rub her palms together is the first physical directive that demonstrates compliance and a willingness to accept and follow the preceding suggestions. Mentioning how the hands will immediately begin getting warm as she rubs them together is a suggestion that will take place because the friction creates heat. Asking her in a persuading way, if she feels the heat radiating from her hands, covertly instructs her to answer affirmatively. Adding the second and third directives to close the eyelids and to imagine the heat increasing is a persuasive method that causes the physical and mental suggestions to simultaneously take place. The suggestions to *try* and keep rubbing the hands while pressing them together creates friction, increases the heat and the stickiness of the palms, and causes the hand movements to slow down. These suggestions meld the physical action and mental belief together. At this point, conscious awareness has lessened and selective thinking has taken place. The critical faculty has been bypassed, and the subconscious mind is now accepting the suggestions for the hands to meld, stick, and seal together. Having the subject fail at separating the hands demonstrates and proves that she is hypnotized. The final suggestion to notice the downward movement of the arms reaffirms to both you and the subject that she is going deeper into hypnosis.

To reiterate, the fast movement of the hands creates a domino effect. Quickly rubbing the hands together causes friction and warms the hands. It also tires and weakens the arms assisting in slowing the hands down and helping her to fail at separating them. And lastly, it causes the arms and hands to succumb to gravity.

EYE EXERCISE INDUCTION

Introduction:

Following simple instructions is a key component for getting hypnotized. Let's see how well the subject can focus, pay attention, and follow orders.

Induction:

Tell the subject to close her eyelids and listen to what you are about to say. "When I say open, you'll open your eyelids and when I say close, you'll close your eyelids. When I say stare, you'll stare. When I say up, down, right, or left, you'll move your eyeballs up, down, to the right, or to the left. When I say sleep you'll relax deeply and completely, okay?" The moment she responds in the affirmative begin by telling her to open her eyelids by saying open. With her eyes open, point to something and tell her to stare. After a few seconds have her inhale. When exhaling have her close her eyelids by saying, "Close." A few seconds after she closes her eyelids slowly say, "Relax... and sleep... sleep... deep, deep, relaxing sleep when I say open... sleep when I say close... sleep when I say stare... sleep when I say up... sleep when I say down go deeper and deeper to sleep with every breath in... and every breath out... go deeper and deeper to sleep... sleep... deep, relaxing, comfortable, sleep." Now have her open her eyes by saying, "Open." After she opens her eyelids immediately blurt out in succession "Stare... close... stare...

open... stare... left... right... sleep... open... stare... up... close... sleep... stare... close... up... relax... open and sleep... sleep... deep, deep, relaxing sleep when I say open... sleep when I say close... sleep when I say stare... sleep when I say up... sleep when I say down go deeper and deeper to sleep with every breath in... and every breath out... go deeper and deeper to sleep... sleep... deep, relaxing, comfortable, sleep. Relax... and sleep... sleep... deep, deep, relaxing sleep when I say open... sleep when I say close... sleep when I say stare... sleep when I say up... sleep when I say down go deeper and deeper to sleep with every breath in... and every breath out... go deeper and deeper to sleep... sleep... deep, relaxing, comfortable, sleep... open... stare... close... stare... open... stare... left... right... sleep... open... stare... up... close... sleep... stare... close... up... relax... open and sleep... sleep... deep, deep, relaxing sleep when I say open... sleep when I say close... sleep when I say stare... sleep when I say up... sleep when I say down go deeper and deeper to sleep with every breath in... and every breath out... go deeper and deeper to sleep... sleep... deep, relaxing, comfortable, sleep."

Explanation:

Eye closure prevents all outside stimuli from being seen. It also allows the subject to relax and completely focus on your voice and instructions. The instructions set the foundation for everything that is about to take place. You clearly explained what is expected of her and when she acknowledges that she understands her role, the suggestions will be followed with ease and zero resistance. When the clear instructions begin they will quickly become less clear, creating slight confusion which will cause the subject to pay closer attention. At some point, she may possibly internally question what to do. Having her stare and then sleep insinuates that she is to close her eyelids. Having her open her eyelids and sleep implies she is to sleep with her eyelids open. She could also interpret it to mean, close the eyelids and sleep. The successive blurting out of each directive doesn't allow her much room to adjust or figure out what to do, instead, it confuses and overwhelms the mind. Hearing the directives to sleep and relax releases the tension and allows hypnosis to take place. The speediness of the commands at the beginning of the induction accompanies the confusing directions leaving no room to consciously react. The slow, melodic suggestions towards the end of the induction, guides her deeper into hypnosis.

STICKY KNEES INDUCTION

Introduction:

Like the adhesive qualities of tape, sealants, paste, and glue, this induction includes an adhesive bond strong enough to induce hypnosis.

Induction:

While the subject is sitting and staring at both of her knees, have her extend her hands out in front of her, palms facing downward with her arms bent at the elbows. Tell her to loosely spread her fingers apart leaving the hands slightly cupped, as you help adjust them. Once adjusted, pay particular attention to one hand and tell her to tighten and lock her fingers in that position. With conviction place that hand on her knee, pressing the palm and fingers securely against the knee so that her hand encompasses it completely as you dramatically say with fervor, "Stick!" After spending a few seconds pressing and securing her fingers and entire palm firmly to her knee, direct your attention to her other hand. Again, adjust the loosely spread fingers. Have her tighten and lock them in place, and with passion place her hand on her other knee. Press the palm and fingers securely against it so that her hand encompasses her entire knee as you authoritatively say, "Stick!" Spend a few seconds pressing and securing her fingers and entire hand firmly to her knee. Once completed, tell her that her hands are stuck to her knees and that she cannot remove them. Tell her to try. The moment she struggles to remove her hands from her knees, command her to sleep.

Explanation:

The subject's unwavering focus on her knees as you assist in adjusting the fingers, increases the anticipation of being hypnotized. Stiffening and locking her fingers while her hand is still in the air gives her a feeling of immobility. The tightened muscles in her fingers, hands, wrists, arms, elbows, and shoulders, along with the hands pressing tightly against her knees, helps keep the arms in the locked position. This makes it difficult for her to remove the hands from her knees.

Your enthusiasm, confidence, and authoritative manner helps to mold her belief in your abilities. Touching, adjusting, assertively pressing, and commanding the hands to stick to her knees all contribute to bypassing the critical faculty. Giving the order to try and release the hands and successfully failing to do so produces the hypnotic phenomena that enables hypnosis to occur. Suggesting her to sleep prompts her to relinquish all physical attempts to release her hands from her knees and allows her to fully relax her body and mind.

ARM CRAWLING INDUCTION

Introduction:

This induction starts out as a handshake and quickly turns into something that you help conjure up in the subject's mind. Imagine expecting one thing and getting something totally different. What type of reaction would you express - creepy, funny, paralyzing, or maybe hypnotic? Let's see.

Induction:

As you reach out to shake the subject's hand, with both of your hands, grasp her hand with your right hand and use the fingers of your left hand to crawl up her arm, starting from her wrist all the way up to her face. The moment your hand touches her face, command her to sleep.

The moment your left hand begins its trek up her arm, you can begin blurting out suggestions to cause an emotive reaction. Four examples of things to blurt out would be, "Look at the creepy crawling spider and sleep!" or "Notice the tickling sensation moving up your arm as it causes you to giggle and sleep!" Another one is, "Look at your arm as it stiffens. Tighten your arm, clench your hand and sleep!" and finally, "Notice how each movement up your arm causes you to go deeply to sleep!" These are four different ways of doing this induction. Choose one of the four ways from the options below.

One:

When crawling up the subject's arm with the creepy crawling spider, the suggestion, "Look at the creepy crawling spider and sleep!" the finger movements, and the hand movement to her face should be wildly quick. The moment the subject displays a reaction to what's happening, immediately cover her face with your hand and command her to sleep.

Two:

With the tickling sensation, your objective is to make the subject smile or giggle. Your suggestive tone when saying, "Notice the tickling sensation moving up your arm as it causes you to giggle and sleep!" and the way you move your fingers up and around her arm as if you are tickling her, should cause her to positively react. The moment she smiles or giggles, immediately place your hand on her face and command her to sleep.

Three:

Move your hand up and along her arm checking it for tautness as you continuously tell her it is becoming stiff, rigid, and solid like a steel bar. While suggesting arm catalepsy, persuade the subject to clench your hand as her arm tightens, and include the following, "Look at your arm as it stiffens. Tighten your arm, clench your hand, and sleep!" The moment you feel her tighten her grip, touch her face and command her to sleep.

Four:

With all of the above suggestions, the word "sleep" should be said when your hand reaches the subject's face. With the exception of this fourth suggestion, you can continue persuading her to sleep by saying, "Notice how each movement up your arm causes you to go deeply to sleep!" This is said in a more relaxed tone as your left hand slowly moves forward and backward and up and around her arm. When her eyelids close, continue the slow movement upward, and when you reach her face tell her to go into a deep relaxing hypnotic sleep.

Explanation:

The first and second examples given, focuses on the emotive reactions being displayed. The moment the subject expresses the emotion of fear or laughter, is when you interrupt the panicky or amused reactions by giving the command to sleep. Emotions are the language of the subconscious mind, therefore when the subject becomes emotional she is in a suggestive state.

The third example is creating hypnotic phenomena via your suggestions. When the subject believes that her arm is stiff and rigid like a steel bar, and she demonstrates that she cannot move or bend it, she is technically hypnotized and ready for your suggestions. The fourth example creates relaxation by convincing her that she is calm, tired, sleepy, and experiencing fatigue and peacefulness with each deliberately slow movement of your hand traveling up her arm.

THIS HAND / THAT HAND INDUCTION

Introduction:

If you would love to learn a slow or quick, powerful, fascinating induction, raise your right hand for slow, your left hand for fast, and two hands for both.

Induction:

Have the subject put her hands up in front of her face and tell her to look at one of her palms. Tell her that once she picks a point on her hand, she is to focus her full attention on it. Once you observe her focusing intently, tell her to look at her other hand and focus on a different spot. Once she has done so tell her to turn her hands over and have her focus on a point on the back of one of the hands. After observing her focusing intently, tell her to stare at the other hand and focus.

Now that she knows what to do, slowly begin to speed up your instructions and have her look at one of the hands and then the other. Have her turn one hand over and flip it back and tell her to look at the other hand and then the other hand and then the back or the front of one of the hands and so forth. The moment she appears to be confused command her to sleep.

Explanation:

Slowly and calmly explaining what to do gives the subject the confidence in following your directions, and her fixation of attention helps to move her toward trance. Now that you've built up her confidence, increase the speed. Shortly after, make her believe she isn't accurately following some of your instructions by frantically overly correcting her. After you've purposely added a little tension and confusion, this should cause her to feel distressed and thankful when you quell the chaos by commanding her to sleep.

BE CAREFUL INDUCTION

Introduction:

As previously and often mentioned, the safety of the client is a top priority - especially in this case!

Induction:

Ask the subject to move from one side of you to the other side. The moment she begins walking, abruptly exclaim, "Watch it!" as you point your finger in the direction beside or behind her. This action will startle her and prompt her to quickly look in that direction or it will cause her to move away from that area. The moment she fearfully reacts will be the moment you command her to sleep.

Explanation:

The key to this induction is to catch the subject off guard by making her believe the induction hasn't begun yet even though the moment you ask her to move from point A to B is when the induction actually starts. Your verbal concern for her safety will surprise her by causing her to freeze, quickly look in the direction of danger, or retreat away from the potentially dangerous area. This moment of fear is enough to bypass the critical faculty. It is at this precise moment your command for her to sleep is all that is needed to thrust her into hypnosis.

HAND & EYE INDUCTION

Introduction:

This is a simple and creative rapid technique that surprisingly confuses the subject, clearly causing a display of bafflement. This will indicate to you that your opportunity to swiftly induce hypnosis is imminent.

Induction:

Stand in front of the sitting subject slightly off to her right. Utilizing both of your hands, manipulate her right hand and arm, keeping the arm bent at the elbow with the forearm straight up and down, perpendicular to your body. With the elbow facing the floor and the fingertips of the opened hand pointing towards the ceiling, turn the hand so that the palm is facing her. Once the arm and hand are in position, the hand should be adjusted approximately nine inches in front of her face at eye level. While lightly holding the back of her right wrist with your right hand, point your left index finger at her palm. Nearly touching the palm with the tip of your finger, simultaneously say, "Look!..." The moment she looks at her palm complete the sentence, "... at my left eye." As soon as she attempts to look at your left eye, while staring directly at her, induce hypnosis by quickly shouting out the "sleep" command.

Explanation:

While standing slightly to the right but in front of the sitting subject, give simple directives such as, "Sit comfortably with your feet flat on the floor and follow my instructions." As you quietly manipulate her right arm and hand, she will be watching and keeping her arm and hand loose and limp so as to not struggle with you. If she is tense, simply direct her to relax. She doesn't know what you are trying to do so she is paying close attention, complying with your non-verbal movements of her hand placement, and waiting for your instructions. Satisfied with the position of her hand, concentration, compliance, and built up expectation, you are ready to deliver the command that will ultimately confuse her. At the right moment when you point and settle your finger close to her palm, firmly give the order, "Look!...", implying that she should look at the palm of her right hand. The moment she believes that she should be looking at her palm, she will physically begin to look. The moment the subject looks at her palm, immediately continue your directive, completing the sentence by saying, "...at my left eye." This command causes the subject to experience her first moment of confusion. Continue watching her face as you look for signs of puzzlement to appear. You're waiting for her to take her eyes off of her right hand because you know that the second set of confusion is about to immediately follow and baffle her once again, as she hurriedly looks up and tries to determine which eye to look at. It is within this brief moment of confusion that you authoritatively shout out the command, "Sleep!" and immediately follow up with a deepener.

CLAP INDUCTION (VERSION II)

Introduction:

If you found the (Clap induction version I) interesting, this sneaky sequel should bring you satisfaction as well.

Induction:

Have the subject stand or sit in front of you with her hands down by her sides or on her lap. As you instruct her to stare into your eyes, smoothly, yet quickly take hold of her wrists and lift her hands upward near her head while saying, "Put your hands up here, just like this." While completing the sentence, her right hand should be simultaneously placed slightly above the right side of her head as her left hand is placed slightly above the left side of her head. As you redirect her attention by having her continue staring into your eyes, along with inhaling and exhaling, slowly and inconspicuously release her wrists. The moment you release your grasps and her arms remain in position, forcefully clap your hands together in front of her face while commanding her to sleep.

Explanation:

Having the subject sit or stand and stare into your eyes, along with focusing on inhaling and exhaling are ways to distract her attention away from her hands. The slow, inconspicuous release of her wrists causes her unsupported arms and hands to remain floating in the air. This brief moment of her being unaware of her unattended hands gives you the opportunity to shock her into hypnosis. Quickly bringing your hands down in front of her face, loudly clapping them together, and commanding her to sleep, completes the procedure.

ARM WRITING INDUCTION

Introduction:

As you write the instruction on the subject's arm, watch how easily she enters hypnosis.

Induction:

Position the subject's arm so that her palm is facing slightly upward. Have her focus her attention on the inner part of her arm as you explain how you will trace the word sleep on it with your finger. Tell her that her eyelids will get heavy and close as she continues to focus on the word sleep. As you slowly and repeatedly trace the word sleep, inform her that her eyelids are becoming heavy and tired with each letter that you write. Tell her they are beginning to close as she goes deeply to sleep.

Explanation:

The subject's fixated attention on her arm along with the suggestions of eye fatigue, eye closure, and the added kinesthetic touch, is enough to cause her to quickly enter hypnosis. Pacing is important. Slowly tracing each letter and bombarding her with suggestions of relaxation, heaviness of the eyelids, deep shallow breathing, and eye closure will influence her to believe and follow the suggestions.

MESMERIZING HANDS INDUCTION

Introduction:

When captivating the subject's complete attention, hypnosis transpires.

Induction:

Put your hands together and place them in front of you as though you are praying. Make sure the fingertips are pointing in the direction of the subject standing or sitting in front of you. Begin rubbing your palms against each other back and forth sliding the right hand forward towards the subject while moving the left hand closer to you and vice versa. While continually alternating the hand movements, have the subject do the same by saying to her, "I want you to rub your hands together like this." The moment the subject starts to rub her hands together, continue on by saying, "Look at my hands as they float." Immediately but slowly separate your hands and move them upward between both of your faces slightly above her eye level. Your fingers should be spread apart and your palms should be facing the subject as your left hand moves from left to right and your right hand moves right to left. Continuously alternate both hands outward towards the sides of the body and inward towards the center of the body, methodically passing each other in a mesmerizing fashion. As you continue on with the suggestions of eye fatigue, let your hands rise a little higher, and then eventually downward towards her chin area. When you see the subject's eyes begin to close, move both hands up towards her face. Cover her eyes, envelop her face, and gently sway her head from side to side while coaxing her to sleep. Complete the induction by saying, "Relax your eyes and sleep... sleep... deep, wonderful, relaxing sleep."

Explanation:

Having the subject focus on your directions to rub her hands together as you demonstrate how she should do it, is a way to capture her attention before interrupting it. The task of rubbing her palms together will immediately be forgotten as she becomes enthralled by your hand movements. The surprise of touching her face, covering her eyes, softly rocking her head side to side, and quietly suggesting she sleep, undoubtedly will send her into hypnosis.

IMAGINE INDUCTION

Introduction:

Imagine being hypnotized, while being hypnotized, while imagining you are imagining being hypnotized.

Induction:

Read this induction aloud slowly or quickly or with variable rhythm. Say some words in one ear and some words in the other ear, or say all the words in both ears simultaneously. Stand beside, behind, or in front of the subject as she focuses on an object slightly above her eyes.

Imagine you are hypnotized...

Imagine you are hypnotized and your eyes are open...

Imagine you are hypnotized and your eyes are open and you can hear my voice...

Imagine you are hypnotized and your eyes are open and you can hear my voice, as you breathe...

Imagine you are hypnotized and your eyes are open or closed and you can hear my voice, as you breathe... as you go deeper into hypnosis...

Imagine you are hypnotized and your eyes are open or closed and you can hear my voice, as you breathe... as you go deeper into hypnosis... imagine your eyes are closed...

Imagine you are hypnotized and your eyes are closed and you can hear my voice, as you breathe... as you go deeper into hypnosis... imagine your eyes are closed... as you imagine you are hypnotized...

Imagine you are hypnotized and your eyes are closed and you can hear my voice, as you breathe... as you go deeper into hypnosis... imagine your eyes are closed... as you imagine you are hypnotized... imagine going deeper into hypnosis now...

Imagine you are hypnotized and your eyes are closed and you can hear my voice, as you breathe... as you go deeper into hypnosis...imagine your eyes are closed... as you imagine you are hypnotized... imagine going deeper into hypnosis now... as you breathe...

Imagine you are hypnotized and your eyes are closed and you can hear my voice, as you breathe... as you go deeper into hypnosis... imagine your eyes are closed... as you imagine you are hypnotized... imagine going deeper into hypnosis now... as you breathe... imagine your legs are so relaxed...

Imagine you are hypnotized and your eyes are closed and you can hear my voice, as you breathe... as you go deeper into hypnosis... imagine your eyes are closed... as you imagine you are hypnotized... imagine going deeper into hypnosis now... as you breathe... imagine your legs are so relaxed... that your stomach is relaxed now...

Imagine you are hypnotized and your eyes are closed and you can hear my voice, as you breathe... as you go deeper into hypnosis... imagine your eyes are closed... as you imagine you are hypnotized... imagine going deeper into hypnosis now... as you breathe... imagine your legs are so relaxed... that your stomach is relaxed - now... your chest is relaxed...

Imagine you are hypnotized and your eyes are closed and you can hear my voice, as you breathe... as you go deeper into hypnosis... imagine your eyes are closed... as you imagine you are hypnotized... imagine going deeper into hypnosis now... as you breathe... imagine your legs are so relaxed... that your stomach is relaxed now... your chest is relaxed... now imagine your arms are relaxed...

Imagine you are hypnotized and your eyes are closed and you can hear my voice, as you breathe... as you go deeper into hypnosis... imagine your eyes are closed... as you imagine you are hypnotized... imagine going deeper into hypnosis now... as you breathe... imagine your legs are so relaxed... that your stomach is relaxed now... your chest is relaxed... now imagine your arms are relaxed... and imagine your eyes, ears, nose, mouth, jaw, lips, face, and head are relaxed...

Imagine you are hypnotized and your eyes are closed and you can hear my voice, as you breathe... as you go deeper into hypnosis... imagine your eyes are closed... as you imagine you are hypnotized... imagine going deeper into hypnosis now... as you breathe... imagine your legs are so relaxed... that your stomach is relaxed now... your chest is relaxed... now imagine your arms are relaxed... as your lower and upper back relaxes... and imagine your eyes, ears, nose, mouth, jaw, lips, face, and head are relaxed... now your whole body is so relaxed, so deeply relaxed because you are now hypnotized just as you imagined being hypnotized.

Explanation:

Reading this script aloud in a monotonous tone, while emphasizing certain words or sentences, and even adding slight pauses and sometimes speeding up and slowing down the pace, is a surefire way to bypass the critical faculty. The inculcation and compounding of the suggestions is the top secret method that lets the subconscious mind do its magic.

SENSORY PACING INDUCTION

Introduction:

If you can breathe, swallow, blink, twitch, or relax, then you can get hypnotized.

Induction:

Relay to the subject that she will notice many things happening to her body like the twitching of her limbs and eyelids, changes in her breathing, swallowing, eye lacrimation, muscle fatigue, and many other things both physically and physiologically. Tell her that as these things occur you will monitor and notify her of every detail as she continues to relax and drift into a deep hypnotic rest. You can begin the process by slowly stating, "I'm noticing and I wonder if you notice how you're breathing - when you inhale and when you exhale - and even when you pause in between breaths." Continue mentioning everything you notice thereafter and have her place her attention on these things as you give her suggestions to relax her body and mind. Convince her to notice that everything you mention and make her aware of is actually causing her to go into hypnosis. When her eyelids close or are nearly closed have her imagine she is hypnotized.

Explanation:

Mentioning the truisms of muscle twitching, swallowing, blinking, feeling tired, relaxing, and even going into hypnosis is in and of itself the process used to hypnotize someone. The pauses you take when there appears to be moments of nothing happening and your inhalation and exhalation or yawning, are things you can use to temporarily shift from pacing to leading. Instead of responding to her actions, cause her to respond to your actions. At this time suggestions of eye closure along with the appearance of your eyelids struggling to stay open can be used. Utilizing the words, "That's right" after the subject twitches or deeply breathes or makes a sudden movement, allows her to mentally acknowledge that something major just occurred and that she is doing exactly what she should be doing to go into hypnosis.

THE HUMAN HAND INDUCTION

Introduction:

The hand is described as a grasping organ at the end of our forelimb. It's made up of vertebrates with digits, a medial thumb, and a wrist which all have great mobility and flexibility, making it a great device to produce hypnosis.

Induction:

In a moment you are going to have the subject place her hand approximately ten inches in front of her face and have her look at it as you explain the importance of having thumbs. Mention the lines, knuckles, fingers, nails, etcetera. Eventually, have her briefly focus on a particular point and then tell her to close her eyelids and imagine that she is still focusing on that part of her hand. Talk about how intense focus on something makes it much easier to notice different types of sensations like when a breeze moves across her hand as it floats in the air. Tell her she may even notice herself drifting deeply into hypnosis as her hand slowly drops downward. As her hand begins to move tell her to drop deeper and deeper down with every movement, breath, and sound of your voice.

Now have her position her hand near her face and stare at it as you start describing the parts of it in an educational, tedious fashion.

"Take a look at the skin on your hand. The web of your hand is a fold of skin that connects each digit and they are called interdigital folds. The skin on your palm is less movable and thicker than the skin on the back of your hand whereas the skin on the back of your hand is thin and freely moveable. Notice what happens when you focus all of your attention on a point on the back of your hand. Focus your attention on that area with minimal blinking and soon you will notice how relaxed you become as you close your eyelids now. Imagine that you are still looking at that area on the back of your hand.

Did you know that there are twenty-seven bones in the hand? An x-ray of the hands can reveal the approximate age of a person and the bones in the thumb are called phalanges while each of the fingers are called digits. It's amazing how the complex movements of the fingers allow us to write, hold items, point at objects, play instruments, and so many other things. It's even more surprising to me that there are no muscles in the fingers. All the finger movements are controlled by the muscles in the palm and forearm which are connected to the tendons in the fingers. The thumb is the first finger of the hand and it is smaller than the other fingers and further away from them. It is an essential part of our hand because it allows us to grasp things and pick up small objects. Without the thumb, it would be very difficult to write, tie our shoelaces, button our shirts, bathe, shave, cook, and do so many other everyday activities. The thumb is controlled by three major nerves and five hand muscles and it can move in six different directions. It also has three knuckles, the third located near the wrist called the carpometacarpal.

Focusing on something makes it much easier to notice different types of sensations like when a breeze moves across the hand as it floats in the air. You may even notice how it causes you to drift deeply into hypnosis as it slowly drops down towards your lap. Notice how you drift deeper and deeper down with every movement. Drop deeper and deeper to sleep with every breath that you take. Go deeper and deeper down... down... down... with every word that I say. Go deeper and deeper to sleep... sleep...

deep... relaxing... wonderful... restful... sleep... sleep... deeper and deeper to sleep. With every breath that you take go deeper and deeper down... down... down. With every word that I say go deeper and deeper to sleep... sleep... deep... relaxing... wonderful... restful... sleep... sleep... sleep... all the way down."

Explanation:

Boredom is a great tool to cause drowsiness and eventually hypnosis. The more technical and boring you make the discussion of the hand, the more tired, dreary, and sleepy the subject will become. Once you notice her attention span wearing thin, concentrate on directing her to relax and drift into hypnosis.

Having the subject's hand levitate in front of her as you carry on with the monotonous details about the hand, gradually tires the arm. Having her focus her attention on a point on her hand with minimal blinking, increases heaviness and fatigue of the eyelids. A subtle whisk of your hand near her hand will create a breeze. Create the breeze when mentioning how intense focus causes her to notice the sensation of the breeze. This can further move her in the direction of becoming hypnotized because if she imagines that she felt the breeze, she can imagine that she is becoming hypnotized. And lastly, as her hand moves downward, your suggestions to drift deeper into hypnosis are followed.

THE INVISIBLE WORD INDUCTION

Introduction:

A positive hallucination is when you hear, smell, taste, feel, or see something that is not present. A negative hallucination is when you cannot hear, smell, taste, feel, or see something that is present. The invisible becomes visible or the visible becomes invisible as in this induction.

Induction:

To do this induction use the words on the back cover of this book. Tell the subject that you are going to have her look for a word. Mention that some people easily find the word while others have more difficulty finding it. You can tell the story about how one person found the word in less than five seconds while another took five minutes to find it, and another person could not find the word at all.

Begin by stating, "Printed on the back of this book are a group of words. I'm going to say a word and have you search for it. While searching for it, continue repeating the word in your mind. The moment you find the word, place your finger on it, okay? While you are looking for the word I will try to distract you by continually talking to you, but feel free to consciously ignore the distraction of my voice, okay? Before we begin I'll give you a couple of words to look for so you will get a feel of what to expect, alright? And also, just know that some words may take five seconds to find while others may take several minutes or longer. Ready?" Once she is ready, have her look for the word *hypnosis*. Say, "Go!" and make it a point to distract her with small talk about hypnosis. After she locates the word, praise her for the brief amount of time it took, and then have her search for the word *sleep*. Say, "Go!" As she begins her search, talk about the differences between sleep and hypnosis and how both are used to alleviate stress. When she locates the word, praise her for successfully finding it, and get her prepared to search for the word *bed-wetter*. This time give her a time limit of forty-five seconds to find the word. The moment she begins her search, begin the timed hypnosis patter below.

"It's funny how some words take five seconds to find while others take several minutes or longer. You easily found the word hypnosis just like you easily found the word - **sleep when I point to the word.** Each stressful second leaves you to believe that **you cannot find the word as you continue to ignore me. The moment I point the word out** to **you will smirk or giggle and maybe even laugh or respond in some way.** Laughter helps release stress. Because laughter is an emotion and emotions are the language of the subconscious mind, **the moment you laugh or respond when I say sleep, your eyelids will close - and you will instantly enter a deep hypnotic sleep - when I point to the word and say bed-wetter - go into hypnosis when I say sleep.**"

The moment you finish the above patter, quickly point to the word and say, **"*Enuresis* is another word for *bed-wetter*."** Immediately during her response, whether she smirks, giggles, or laughs, quickly place your other hand on her shoulder. At the same time move your hand away from the word towards her face and snap your fingers, as you command her to, **"sleep!"**

Explanation:

Easily finding the two words at her convenience builds the subject's confidence, and adding a time limit with the third word creates hastiness. This also sets her up to engage in panic mode or at least adds a little pressure as each second elapses while she's mentally repeating and visually searching for the third word. Any internal dialogue or feelings of frustration, uneasiness, or angst causes her to consciously disregard your patter, which is filled with suggestions to go into hypnosis. Even though she is trying to consciously ignore you while attempting to remain focused on finding the word, her subconscious mind is listening and preparing to follow your suggestions to go into hypnosis on your command.

The following is a breakdown of the commands in bold text within the above patter.

Sleep when I point to the word.

You cannot find the word as you continue to ignore me.

The moment I point the word out, you will smirk or giggle and maybe even laugh or respond in some way.

The moment you laugh or respond when I say sleep, your eyelids will close and you will instantly enter a deep hypnotic sleep.

You will instantly enter a deep hypnotic sleep when I point to the word and say bed-wetter.

When I point to the word and say bed-wetter, go into hypnosis.

When I say sleep go into hypnosis.

Go into hypnosis when I say sleep.

Enuresis is another word for bed-wetter.

Sleep!

Note:

The subject should not be privy to the words on the back cover of the book beforehand. Any familiarity with the words may interfere with the success of the induction.

Place the book on the table with the front cover facing up. Turn the book over when you are ready to have the subject search for the word.

When reading the above patter, emphasize the bold words by slightly deepening your voice so that the words are projected as a command.

Enuresis is the involuntary discharge of urine - incontinence of urine.

Nocturnal enuresis or nighttime incontinence is involuntary urination while sleeping.

Below are other words within the group of words on the back cover of the book that can be used instead of the word *bed-wetter*.

Bruxism is a medical condition characterized as grinding or clenching of the teeth. Tell the subject to look for the words, *teeth grinding*.

Insomnia is a sleep disorder where you have trouble falling asleep and or staying asleep. Tell the subject to look for the words, *racing thoughts*, which is something an insomniac experiences when trying to sleep.

Teeth Grinding Patter:

Begin by stating, "Printed on the back of this book are a group of words. I'm going to say a word and have you search for it. While searching for it, continue repeating the word in your mind. The moment you find the word, place your finger on it, okay? While you are looking for the word I will try to distract you by continually talking to you, but feel free to consciously ignore the distraction of my voice, okay? Before we begin I'll give you a couple of words to look for so you will get a feel of what to expect, alright? And also, just know that some words may take five seconds to find while others may take several minutes or longer. Ready?" Once she is ready, have her look for the word *hypnosis*. Say, "Go!" and make it a point to distract her with small talk about hypnosis. After she locates the word, praise her for the brief amount of time it took, and then have her search for the word *sleep*. Say, "Go!" As she begins her search, talk about the differences between sleep and hypnosis and how both are used to alleviate stress. When she locates the word, praise her for successfully finding it, and get her prepared to search for the words *teeth grinding*. This time give her a time limit of forty-five seconds to find the word. The moment she begins her search, begin the timed hypnosis patter below.

"It's funny how some words take five seconds to find while others take several minutes or longer. You easily found the word hypnosis just like you easily found the word - **sleep when I point to the word.** Each stressful second leaves you to believe that **you cannot find the word as you continue to ignore me. The moment I point the word out** to **you will smirk or giggle and maybe even laugh or respond in some way.** Laughter helps release stress. Because laughter is an emotion and emotions are the language of the subconscious mind, **the moment you laugh or respond when I say sleep, your eyelids will close - and you will instantly enter a deep hypnotic sleep - when I point to the words and say *teeth grinding* - go into hypnosis when I say sleep."**

The moment you finish the above patter, quickly point to the word and say, **"Bruxism is another word for *teeth grinding*."** Immediately during her response, whether she smirks, giggles, or laughs, quickly place your other hand on her shoulder. At the same time move your hand away from the word towards her face and snap your fingers, as you command her to, **"sleep!"**

Racing Thoughts Patter:

Begin by stating, "Printed on the back of this book are a group of words. I'm going to say a word and have you search for it. While searching for it, continue repeating the word in your mind. The moment you find the word, place your finger on it, okay? While you are looking for the word I will try to distract you by continually talking to you, but feel free to consciously ignore the distraction of my voice, okay? Before we begin I'll give you a couple of words to look for so you will get a feel of what to expect, alright? And also, just know that some words may take five seconds to find while others may take several minutes or longer. Ready?" Once she is ready, have her look for the word *hypnosis*. Say, "Go!" and make it a point to distract her with small talk about hypnosis. After she locates the word, praise her for the brief amount of time it took, and then have her search for the word *sleep*. Say, "Go!" As she begins her search, talk about the differences between sleep and hypnosis and how both are used to alleviate stress. When she locates the word, praise her for successfully finding it, and get her prepared to search for the words *racing thoughts*. This time give her a time limit of forty-five seconds to find the word. The moment she begins her search, begin the timed hypnosis patter below.

"It's funny how some words take five seconds to find while others take several minutes or longer. You easily found the word hypnosis just like you easily found the word - **sleep when I point to the word.** Each stressful second leaves you to believe that **you cannot find the word as you continue to ignore me. The moment I point the word out** to **you will smirk or giggle and maybe even laugh or respond in some way.** Laughter helps release stress. Because laughter is an emotion and emotions are the language of the subconscious mind, **the moment you laugh or respond when I say sleep, your eyelids will close - and you will instantly enter a deep hypnotic sleep - when I point to the words and say** *racing thoughts* - **go into hypnosis when I say sleep."**

The moment you finish the above patter, quickly point to the word and say, **"Insomnia is another word for *racing thoughts*."** Immediately during her response, whether she smirks, giggles, or laughs, quickly place your other hand on her shoulder. At the same time move your hand away from the word towards her face and snap your fingers, as you command her to, **"sleep!"**

HANDSHAKE / ARM INDUCTION

Introduction:

This sneaky induction allows you the opportunity to visually gauge the subject's transition into hypnosis by monitoring her arm movement.

Induction:

Reach out to shake the subject's hand with your right hand, but instead, bypass her hand and grab her wrist. Simultaneously grab the tricep area of her arm just above her elbow with your left hand. Immediately move her arm upward so that her hand is positioned near your shoulder. Slowly release her arm leaving it to float on its own as you say, "Look at that arm floating..." Using your right hand, point to her left arm and say, "...and notice that you cannot lift this arm..." Tap her left forearm closer to the wrist area as you continue on with the sentence by saying, "...because it is so heavy..." Point to the right arm while completing the sentence by saying, "...because that arm is floating." Press down on her left shoulder, and say, "Try and lift this arm - you can't." The moment she struggles to lift her arm, snap your fingers next to her face as you authoritatively say, "Sleep!" Follow up by tapping her right wrist with your left hand and say, "Drop down... deeper... down... deeper... down... deeper, down."

Explanation:

When the traditional handshake is interrupted, it causes the subject to momentarily wonder what is happening. This is when you quickly interrupt her internal dialogue before she has a chance to make sense of what is occurring. Grabbing her wrist and arm and placing it elsewhere while telling her to look at the floating arm, creates some confusion. Her arm should remain levitating after slowly releasing it. Identifying the right arm as that arm and the left arm as this arm disassociates those arms from being her arms. Going back and forth and having her momentarily focus on what one arm is doing and what the other arm cannot do increases just enough confusion necessary to dampen her attempt to raise the left arm. Tapping one arm steers her focus away from the other arm, and pressing down on her shoulder when telling her she cannot lift the arm, gives the sensation of heaviness. Any further testing or verbiage to lift the arm isn't necessary. And lastly, tapping her right arm during the deepening process associates the lowering of the arm with going deeper into hypnosis.

CLAP INDUCTION (VERSION III)

Introduction:

If you found the (Clap induction versions I & II) interesting, this sneakier version will equally delight you.

Induction:

Have the subject stand or sit in front of you with her hands down by her sides or on her lap. As you instruct her to stare into your eyes, smoothly, yet quickly take hold of her wrists and lift her hands upward near her head while saying "Put your arms up here just like this." While completing the sentence, her right hand should be placed slightly above the right side of her head while her left hand is simultaneously placed slightly above the left side of her head. Tell her to remove all tension from her hands and arms so that the only thing keeping them from automatically falling to her sides is you holding onto her wrists. Redirect her attention by having her stare into your eyes, along with inhaling and exhaling. When you notice that you are actually preventing her hands and arms from dropping downwards on their own, abruptly release her wrists and forcefully clap your hands together in front of her face while commanding her to freeze. Immediately follow up by covering her face and eyes while calmly telling her to relax and sleep.

Explanation:

Having the subject sit or stand and stare into your eyes, along with focusing on inhaling and exhaling are ways to distract her attention away from her hands. Slightly wiggling her arms from side to side helps to remove any tension and aids you in gauging the looseness and relaxation of the arms. Immediately after letting go of her wrists, clapping your hands together, and telling her to freeze, should cause her arms to instantly stop moving downward on a subconscious level before she has a chance to consciously stop them on her own. Gently placing your hand upon her face, covering her eyes, and calmly telling her to relax and sleep allows her to completely let go.

BLACKOUT INDUCTION

Introduction:

After placing herself in total darkness, the smallest amount of light is all it takes to send the subject into a deep state of hypnosis.

How to cover the eyes:

Have the subject look at her palms and place both of her hands approximately ten inches away from her face. Instruct her to put the sides of her hands and pinkies together. Both hands should be slightly curved. The thumb of the right hand should be on her right side and the thumb of the left hand should be on her left side. Keeping her hands and fingers tightly together, have her place the cupped hands over her eyes, nose, and mouth as she attempts to prevent any light from penetrating the darkness.

Induction:

Have the subject cover her eyes with both hands sealing the fingers together so she is in complete darkness. Have her deeply inhale and exhale three times. Her eyes are to remain open and she is to continually search the darkness for any signs of light. Periodically ask her if she sees any light, and have her nod her head from side to side if no light is detected. The moment she sees the smallest amount of light squeezing through her fingers, have her report it to you by nodding her head up and down. At that moment tell her to imagine her hands, arms, and shoulders relaxing as she continues to breathe. Persuade her to go deeply into hypnosis as the light pierces and consumes the darkness and her fingers separate with each relaxing breath.

Explanation:

The subject's goal is to prevent light from penetrating the darkness, and your objective is to covertly cause light to enter it. Having her deeply inhale and exhale creates the opportunity for light to accidentally enter the darkness. Nodding her head and the suggestions to relax her hands, arms, and shoulders also increases the chances of more light entering the darkness. Encouraging her to nonverbally respond while persuading her to relax, breathe, and constantly look for a minute glimpse of light, is a task that when fulfilled will initiate the hypnosis process.

DÉJÀ VU INDUCTION

Introduction:

Déjà vu is a feeling of having already experienced the present situation. If the subject has never encountered this strange phenomenon before, now you can create it for her.

Induction:

Have the subject stare at something in front of her. While taking a moment to monitor her breaths, tell her to focus and listen to your voice. From this moment on you should be telling her to do everything after the fact. Upon observing her breathing, the moment she inhales immediately tell her to inhale. When she exhales, tell her to exhale. When she blinks, tell her to blink. When she opens her eyelids after blinking, immediately tell her to open her eyes and focus on the object in front of her. While she is focusing on the object and listening to you, tell her to focus and listen to your voice. The moment she starts to inhale immediately tell her to inhale. When she exhales, immediately tell her to exhale. When she blinks, tell her to blink. When she opens her eyelids after blinking, immediately tell her to open her eyes, focus on the object in front of her, and sleep. When she inhales and exhales, tell her to breathe, and listen to your voice as she sleeps and breathes and focuses.

Continue on with the following in the same manner as the aforementioned. Whether the eyes are opened or closed, after each ellipsis, say the following immediately when each blink and breath occurs. "Open your eyes and wake up... now close your eyes and go back to sleep... blink... inhale... exhale... close your eyes now... open your eyes again so you can close them when you blink... and inhale... and exhale again as you sleep... and close your eyes and go deeper than before... deeper to sleep - now."

Explanation:

Déjà vu occurs when you feel like something is familiar to you without actually having experienced it before. With this induction, the attempt is to confuse the subject and purposely cause her to internally question whether she has just breathed, opened her eyes, or focused prior to you telling her to do so. Tell her to do anything that she has already done such as sigh, deeply inhale, exhale, twitch, or anything else. Having her do everything she's already done or experienced, along with telling her to do something she hasn't done yet, such as go to sleep, will eventually confuse her and make it easier for her to go into hypnosis.

HAND OR EYES INDUCTION

Introduction:

Watch how your hand reacts to the subject's eyes and vice versa.

Induction:

With your arm bent at the elbow, fingers close together, and fingertips pointing up towards the ceiling, as though you are about to wave at the subject, tell her to look at your hand and focus her full attention on the center of your palm. Continue on by saying the following, adding a slight pause in between each directive. "Notice your eyes are getting tired... Your eyelids are getting heavy... Notice my fingers curving downward..." Let the fingers slowly begin to curve downward eventually turning into a fist. "As your eyelids close, my fingers close..." As you carefully watch the eyelids close, let your fingers mimic her eye closure movements until both her eyelids and your fist are tightly closed.

Now that the eyelids are closed, the pace and continuance of the following directives will be spoken in a more authoritative and slightly rapid and mechanical manner. "Tighter and tighter - tightly closed - locked. They cannot open. In a moment I'm going to count from one to three and when I reach the number three you'll try and open your eyelids and you'll find that you cannot open them. One, two, and three, try and open those eyelids now. You cannot open them." Once she successfully demonstrates that she cannot open the eyelids, continue on. "That's right. Stop trying now and relax those eyelids and allow that relaxation from those eyelids to flow down your entire body, causing you to relax all over."

Explanation:

You are pretending to mimic the subject's eyelids straining to stay open with your hand movement. Your attempt to convince her that your hand movements are reacting to her eyelids struggling to remain open causes her to think that her eyelids are tired and heavy and closing. In her mind, your hand closure is acting as a mirror image of what her eyes are doing. The truth is *she* is mimicking your hand movements.

THE HYPNOTIC MERIDIAN INDUCTION

Introduction:

Massaging the invisible pathway or meridian that begins at the tip of the middle finger and ends near the inside crease of the arm, opposite the elbow, produces lethargy and deep hypnosis.

Induction:

Begin this induction with an explanation of the invisible meridian or pathway that begins at the tip of the longest finger and stretches within the center of the arm to its endpoint located at the inner crease opposite the elbow. Tell the subject that you are going to place your finger on the tip of her middle finger and slowly move your finger down the arm to the crease where the arm bends. Continue by saying that tracing your finger down her arm causes an extraordinary amount of fatigue to build up. Finish by saying that the moment you release the pressure, the fatigue quickly travels to the subconscious mind instantly inducing hypnosis.

After explaining the technique to the subject, bend and adjust her arm at a 45 degree angle making sure her fingertips are pointing towards the ceiling. While holding the back of her forearm, tell her to stiffen her middle finger and stare at it. Place your finger on the tip of her middle finger and briefly apply a small amount of pressure to it. After you tell her to follow the movement of your finger with her eyes, begin to slowly trace your finger down her finger, palm, wrist, and arm. As you move your finger downward, tell her to notice how the slow movement is beginning to take effect. When you reach the inner crease of her arm, opposite the elbow, apply a little pressure. While applying the pressure continue by saying, "When I release the pressure from your arm, your eyes will close and you will go deeply to sleep." The moment you release the pressure from her arm, you should immediately and quickly tap her arm downward by pressing on the crease of her arm as you authoritatively command her to sleep.

Explanation:

Explaining how tracing the invisible meridian creates lethargy and produces deep hypnosis is a fabrication. Continue the persuasive manufacturing of these hypnotic occurrences until they present themselves. As the subject follows the slow downward movement of your finger, her eyelids are also slowly closing. The next step increases the anticipation of the release of the finger and the expectation of going deeply into hypnosis. When you reach your destination, apply a slight amount of pressure on the crease of the subject's arm and say, "When I release the pressure from your arm, your eyes will close and you will go deeply to sleep." The unexpected surprise of quickly pushing down on her arm after releasing the pressure while commanding her to sleep instantly sends her into hypnosis.

CYCLE OF SLEEP / HYPNOSIS DEPTH INDUCTION

Introduction:

Interweaving the cycles of sleep and the stages of hypnosis produces astonishing results.

Induction:

Have the subject fixate her eyes on an object slightly above eye level, and tell her that you are going to inform her of the cycles of sleep and the different stages of hypnosis. Have her focus on her breaths by having her notice when she inhales, exhales, and pauses, as you read the following to her.

"When falling asleep we go through cycles. Each cycle consists of five stages.

Stage one is light sleep where our muscle activities including our eye movements slow down. During this stage we may experience muscle contractions.

Stage two is also a light sleep and the eye movements stop.

Stages three and four are sometimes combined as stage three. It's a deep state of sleep, and all muscle activity stops.

Stage five is rapid eye movement or REM sleep where we often dream.

With hypnosis, we start out with the beta waves. That's the state that we are in right now. We're alert and consciously aware of what's happening. As you listen to my voice and relax you go into the alpha state which is similar to daydreaming. It's meditative, focused attention. Imagine I'm talking to you and your eyes are open yet all of a sudden your mind drifts off sort of like when you were a child in school looking out of the window, spacing out as the teacher was talking or when you drive and your mind is someplace else. The theta state is that magnificent place where solutions to a problem come to fruition, where you get a sudden insight, where the creative juices flow, where questions are answered, and where things become understood. Think about when something is bothering you and you don't quite know how to handle it and then you go to bed and sleep and when you awaken you know exactly what it is you need to do. And then there's the delta state where the deepest levels of relaxation and restorative healing occurs.

So imagine, for a moment that you're lying in bed. You fluff your pillow and position yourself and get comfortable. You sigh, taking in a deep breath and exhaling all of the day's activities away as you close your eyelids as though they are blinds keeping out all of the light, or doors closing behind you, keeping all outside visual and auditory stimuli away. As you begin your journey inward, your eye movements and muscles are relaxing, and any muscle contractions that you experience moves you deeper down the path of sleep.

Leaving behind the beta waves, and entering into the alpha state, imagine the relaxation from your toes moving upward, relaxing all the muscles and tendons and organs, and cells in your body from the tips of your toes to the top of your head as the blood flows throughout your body and the oxygen fills you with calm, peaceful, serenity. Each breath filling you with tranquility, relaxing all the muscles and tendons and organs, and cells in your body from the tips of your toes to the top of your head as the blood flows throughout your body and the oxygen fills you with calm, peaceful, serenity. Imagine entering and passing through the theta state, that magnificent place where solutions to problems come to fruition, where you get a sudden insight, where the creative juices flow, where questions are answered, and where things become understood.

As we allow the works of the theta state to carry on, imagine entering the delta state, where the deepest levels of relaxation and restorative healing occurs. Imagine, see, and feel the mental, physical and emotional restorative healing occurring now as you continue to relax and go deeper and deeper down... down... down...relaxing... healing... growing... learning... healing... as you go deeper and deeper down... down... down... Imagine and see and feel the mental and physical and emotional restorative healing taking place as you continue to relax and go deeper and deeper down... down... down...relaxing... healing... growing... learning... and healing... as you go deeper and deeper down... down... down..."

[Insert a script and /or emerge the subject from hypnosis by reading the following.]

"Imagine now that you are moving up from the delta state where the restorative healing continues as you move through the theta state where solutions and creativity and confidence, joy, and happiness are attaching themselves to you. As you begin your upward movement towards the relaxing alpha state, take a deep breath filling your lungs with energy and oxygen, and imagine yourself now entering the beta state as you open your eyes now and return to full conscious awareness feeling absolutely magnificent, rejuvenated, invigorated, relaxed and alert."

Explanation:

After talking about the sleep cycles, hypnosis is introduced with the sentence that states, "With hypnosis, we start out with the beta waves." You may prefer to omit the word hypnosis when dealing with a subject who may be overly nervous about hypnosis, or maybe you just want the subject to focus entirely on sleep. Another reason to not mention hypnosis may simply be because you want this to be a disguised induction. To do this, begin the hypnosis commentary portion by saying, "We start out with the beta waves." Adjustments can be made by having the subject close her eyelids so that she can focus entirely on your words without experiencing any outside visual interference.

Visually focusing on a particular object slightly above eye level tires the eyes and encourages eye closure. Focusing on each breath contributes to producing relaxation and diverts the subject's attention away from what's being said, which creates the opportunity for the bypassing of the critical mind. Talking about the cycles of sleep, and interweaving the brainwave information and hypnotic suggestions together, intrigues the subject. The inclusion of the visual imagery, relaxation, hypnosis, deepening of hypnosis, and the emergence from hypnosis, leaves you with a well rounded induction, ready to be used when needed.

OVERLOAD INDUCTION

Introduction:

It has been said that our short term memories can store (seven plus or minus two) chunks of information at any given time. Watch how the subconscious mind reacts when we overload the conscious mind with numerous chunks of information.

Induction:

Shake the subject's hand for volunteering to get hypnotized. Tell her to look into your eyes, take a deep breath, and exhale. Continue shaking her hand until you tell her to sleep. Ask her to give you her other hand as you reach over your linked hands with your left hand and close her hand into a fist. Extend her thumb up towards the ceiling and position her arm so that the tip of her thumb is slightly above eye level. Tell her to look at your eyes, take a deep breath, and exhale. Point to her thumb while telling her to stare at it. Place your hand on her right shoulder close to her neck and look down at her shoes. Tell her to adjust her feet so that they are positioned like yours, as you move your feet closer together or further apart. Firmly remind her to focus on her thumb. Begin tapping the back of her neck quickly and steadily with your index finger as you lean in to relay a set of instructions into her ear. Have her take another deep breath, and stop tapping her neck the moment you begin saying, "The next time I tap the back of your neck I want you to immediately begin counting backwards in your mind, starting from the number ten. As soon as you begin counting, your eyes will close, your head will drop down, your body will become completely relaxed and you will - go into a deep hypnotic - sleep." The moment you give the command to (go into a deep hypnotic sleep), start tapping her neck a few times when you say the first word of the command, "go." As you say the word, "sleep" gently yank her arm and continue with a deepener.

Explanation:

A handshake is used as a formal greeting, a farewell, or to finalize an agreement. When shaking hands, the protocol is to extend your right hand out which is reciprocated by the other person who extends their right hand out to meet yours. Both party's usually clasp each other's hands and move them up and down in unison between one to five times before stopping and releasing their grip. This action lasts approximately two to four seconds. In some instances after the handshaking has ceased, one party may hold the other person's hand for a longer period while engaging in conversation. This particular handshake is in a league of its own.

Shaking hands throughout the entire induction causes the subject's body to continually sway. When told to look into your eyes and to focus on her thumb, this motion, however slightly, makes it impossible for her to remain still. The continual motion causes her to struggle to focus on what should be stationary objects. The kinesthetic touching of the subject's hand and swaying of her body begins the process of overloading her senses.

Having the subject breathe helps her to relax and remain calm. It momentarily shifts her attention elsewhere, giving you another opportunity to make her believe that she is deviating from carrying out a previous task.

Telling her to give you her hand and silently manipulating it by positioning the arm, hand, fingers, and thumb, is another kinesthetic facet used to cause the subject to internally analyze what's going on, while at the same time adding more chunks of data to the load.

Positioning the subject's hand into a fist diverts her attention away from your eyes, to her hand. Reminding her to look at your eyes and to breathe, stresses the point to pay attention, focus, and relax.

Pointing at her thumb and directing her to stare at it as you place your left hand on her right shoulder, stimulates both her visual and kinesthetic senses once again. With your hand on her shoulder, you are able to assist her in making slight adjustments by positioning her body to the right then to the left or vice versa while correcting her feet placement.

You've subjected her to a barrage of instructions accumulating seven - plus two chunks of things to do thus far. Everything from this point on will continue overloading her conscious mind, making it easy for her to surrender to your requests to enter hypnosis.

Telling her to adjust her feet so that they are positioned like yours, causes her to once again take her eyes off of her thumb so she can see how your feet are positioned, so that she can adjust her feet to your liking. This gives you another opportunity to firmly remind her to place her attention on her thumb. By this time she should be internally reminding herself to fixate her full attention on her thumb without succumbing to any more distractions.

Continuously tapping the back of her neck, having her take another deep breath, and even stopping the tapping, all contribute to the overstimulation of her kinesthetic sense. Invading her personal space by stepping closer to her and softly giving her suggestions directly into her ear, has overloaded her with a total of fifteen chunks of directions to follow.

The final suggestions given is a crucial part of the induction where the accumulation of all the other suggestions given are about to come to a head and thrust her into hypnosis. The moment you tap the back of her neck, she will immediately begin mentally counting backwards. This causes her to refocus her attention as you continue with the suggestions. As you tell her everything that is going to happen, the moment you say, "sleep!" simultaneously shock her into hypnosis by gently yanking her arm.

WORD FROM THE AUTHOR

It was a pleasure working on this book and breaking down the mechanics of each induction. I especially enjoyed the inductions from fellow hypnotists I came across on YouTube channels. All but one of their names escapes me and the videos may no longer exist. I cannot give the appropriate credits to these contributors, but I can tell you which inductions within this book, are the ones I once saw being performed by them.

The Standing Hand Press Induction might still be floating around on YouTube.

The Three Handshake Induction has been demonstrated by several hypnotists on YouTube and many of them may still be available for viewing.

The Hypnogenic Points Induction was one of many inductions that the hypnotist was demonstrating in an office setting. I've searched for the videos for quite some time never locating them again.

The Odd/Even Induction is a variant of the Dr. Flowers Induction and might still be floating around on YouTube or elsewhere on the internet.

I saw this Hand-Eye Induction demonstration for the first time in 2012 by its creator, Jeffrey Stephens. Shortly after that, I registered and flew up to New Jersey to partake in his Whole Life Mastery Hypnosis certification class. This rapid induction is still available on Youtube and may possibly be found on the Jeffrey Stephens Hypnosis training website which is hosted by Master Hypnotist Rudy Nooijen, the official successor of the late Jeffrey Stephens.

After being inspired by The Invisible Induction, I created a knock off of it and called it, The Invisible Word Induction.

After seeing this next induction on YouTube where it was being performed on a sidewalk in front of a small group, I coined it The Overload Induction.

Visit:

Website - Life Enriching Hypnosis

YouTube channel - Life Enriching Hypnosis / Hypnotism 101

Meetup - New Bedford Hypnotism 101 Meetup Group

New Bedford Wellness Initiative Facebook page - John Barboza, Hypnotist

The Internet - John Barboza, Hypnotist, Hypnosis, Hypnotism, New Bedford Hypnotist

Trafford Publishing and other electronic formats - Barboza's Book of Hypnotic Inductions

jeffreystephenshypnosis.net - Rudy Nooijen

ABOUT THE AUTHOR

John Barboza became interested in hypnosis at the age of thirteen. The first book he purchased for one dollar, which he still has in his library today, is Hypnotism Revealed by Melvin Powers. After unsuccessful attempts to hypnotize his childhood friends, his interest in hypnosis faded but returned in 2010. After seeing the movie, The Fourth Kind, where hypnotherapy was used throughout the film to uncover possible alien abductions, his desire to learn hypnosis increased with a vengeance. He purchased, read, and accumulated a multitude of books and began hypnotizing hundreds of people, perfecting his craft. Three years later in 2013, he studied under Master Hypnotist, Jeffrey Stephens, and six months later he became a certified consulting hypnotist and member of the National Guild of Hypnotists. Every year thereafter he attended continuing education courses becoming a board certified hypnotist, stage hypnotist, certified instructor, and owner and founder of his private home office hypnotism practice, Life Enriching Hypnosis, located in New Bedford, Massachusetts. He created his Hypnotism 101 YouTube channel in 2019 where he shares his passion for hypnotism with weekly videos that are also posted on the New Bedford Wellness Initiative Facebook page created by Cardiologist, Dr. Michael Rocha. John published a book of short stories in 2006 and Barboza's Book of Hypnotic Inductions in 2020. He is currently working on several other books that he is excited to be releasing in the near future.

Besides hypnosis being his number one passion, John also has several other interests that keep him busy. His other number one passion, equal to hypnosis, is music. John is a singer/songwriter and has recorded and penned several songs that are catalogued on Discogs and are available in many electronic formats including YouTube. He has mentioned that being in a music recording studio where the creative juices flow, makes him feel alive, and doing hypnosis, whether giving a presentation, teaching, or working with a client, fills him with an overwhelming sense of joy. His other interests includes being a member of the Toastmasters club, target shooting, playing and improving his chess game, learning languages, traveling, and taking day tours whenever visiting other states, and most of all, being retired and having the time to enjoy fulfilling his goals and passions.